FINAL CRISIS AFTERMATH

dance

FINAL CRISIS AFTERMATH: DANCE

Joe Casey
Writer

ChrisCross
André Coelho
Eduardo Pansica
Pencillers

Rob Stull
Mick Gray
Wayne Faucher
ChrisCross
André Coelho
Sandro Ribeiro
Marc Deering
Inkers

Snakebite
Pete Pantazis
Colorists

Sal Cipriano
Letterer

Stanley "Artgerm" Lau
Original series cover artist

Cover by Stanley "Artgerm" Lau

FINAL CRISIS AFTERMATH: DANCE

DC Comics, 1700 Broadway, New York, NY 10019
A Warner Bros. Entertainment Company
Printed in World Color Press, Inc.,
St-Romuald, QC, Canada. 3/10/10. First Printing.
ISBN: 978-1-4012-2605-3

Fiber used in this product line meets the sourcing requirements of the SFI program. www.sfiprogram.org PWC-SFICOC-260

CHAPTER ONE
ChrisCross ▮ Penciller
Rob Stull with Mick Gray,
Wayne Faucher & ChrisCross ▮ Inkers

dance

FIFTY-TWO MILES HIGH:
SUPER YOUNG TEAM!
SUSPENSION OF DISBELIEF: ON.

THIS IS HOW WE DO IT
SATELLITE HEADQUARTERS TO THE STARS, HEINO.
EXACTLY.

TIME TO SHOW THE WORLD EXACTLY WHAT WE'RE--
WELCOME ABOARD, GUYS...
...GLAD YOU COULD ALL MAKE IT. AS YOU CAN SEE, STATE-OF-THE-ART ALL THE WAY. MAKES THE JLA'S HALL OF JUSTICE LOOK LIKE GABRIEL'S HORN.
MY NAME IS JUSTIN HANOVER. I'VE BEEN GIVEN THE HONOR TO WORK WITH YOU IN ALL MATTERS OF PUBLIC RELATIONS. Y'KNOW, I STARTED OUT INTERNING AT GOLD-STAR, SO THIS IS RIGHT IN MY WHEELHOUSE.
WE'RE GONNA MAKE SOME SERIOUS NOISE UP IN HERE.
facespace
sourcefield
rumblings
invitations
SUPER YOUNG TEAM'S PROFILE (THIS IS YOU)
ACCOUNT INFO [EDIT]
Name: MOST EXCELLENT SUPERBAT
PERSONAL INFO [EDIT]
Looking For: All that there is
ACCOUNT INFO [EDIT]
Name: BIG ATOMIC LANTERN BOY
PERSONAL INFO [EDIT]
Looking For: Love, attention, devotion
ACCOUNT INFO [EDIT]
Name: SHINY HAPPY AQUAZON
PERSONAL INFO [EDIT]
Looking For: Still looking...
ACCOUNT INFO [EDIT]
Name: SHY CRAZY LOLITA CANARY
PERSONAL INFO [EDIT]
Looking For: Absolution
ACCOUNT INFO [EDIT]
Name: WELL-SPOKEN SONIC LIGHTNING FLASH
PERSONAL INFO [EDIT]
Looking For: Continuous forward motion
MiPhone
VMail
InterWeb
UltraPod

SO, LISTEN... WE'RE ON A BIT OF AN ACCELERATED SCHEDULE HERE. YOU UNDERSTAND. THEY WANT TO GET THINGS STARTED ASAP.
AS THE ACKNOWLEDGED *NEXT GENERATION* OF JAPANESE SUPER-PEOPLE, YOUR WAKING HOURS ARE *BOOKED SOLID*--

--THE POSITIONING HAS TO BE *PERFECT*.
WHAT DO THEY CALL IT? SNAKE-OIL SALESMAN...
PUBLICIST. SAME THING.

BERIGHTBACK.
SO WHO'S *THAT* GUY...?

OH, DON'T WORRY ABOUT MISTER ITAMI. JUST ONE OF THE *INVESTORS* DOING A FINAL ONCE-OVER.
HEY, YOU WANNA DANCE, YOU GOTTA PAY THE BAND. YOU WANNA BORROW, YOU GOTTA PAY THE MAN. I'M NOT EMOTIONALLY INVOLVED.
THISPLACEISTRICKED-OUTTOANINFINITE-DEGREE!
THEY THOUGHT OF *EVERYTHING*... NO CLICHÉ LEFT UNTURNED.
MOST EXCELLENT SUPERBAT. I KNOW YOU'VE GOT YOUR OWN MEANS...BUT WE *FOCUS TESTED* THIS APPROACH.
THE WORLD WANTS ITS HEROES *HUMBLE*. AT LEAST, THEY WANT THEM TO KEEP UP THE PRETENSE.
LET ME SHOW YOU AROUND...
@MOSEXSBAT: AT LEAST THIS FOOL KNOWS I COULD BUY AND SELL HIM.
about 2 seconds ago from Twitteratti

@MOSEXSBAT: THIS IS NOT HOW I WOULD'VE DONE IT. TROPHIES ARE FOR RETIREES. AND BOWLERS.
about 1 minute ago from Twitteratti
...A MONUMENT TO YOUR VAST ACCOMPLISHMENTS. YOUR VICTORIES. YOUR GLORIES. THE SPOILS OF WAR.
FULLY STOCKED FROM TOP TO BOTTOM.
What *is* all this stuff? We don't *have* any spoils...
We should crack open this tequila.
I DON'T RECOGNIZE *ANYTHING* IN HERE...!
I AM SHAMED...
YOU KNOW WE JUST TOOK ON THE ARMIES OF DEATH AND DARKNESS AND *WON*.
WE WERE GUARDIANS OF THE GREAT TUNNEL BETWEEN UNIVERSES. *THAT'S* OUR CLAIM TO FAME.
...FAME IS FLEETING, GUYS. THESE DAYS, YOU'VE GOT TO REINVENT YOURSELVES ONCE A WEEK.
BUT, HEY, CHECK OUT THIS *TRAINING DECK*. THEY TELL ME IT'S BASED ON A S.T.A.R. LABS VIRTUAL COMBAT PROGRAM.
...SHE WON'T EVEN LOOK AT ME.
WOW.
HOW'S IT WORK...?
NO IDEA.
DOES IT MATTER...?
@MOSEXSBAT: MY HOME GYM IS NICER THAN THIS.
about 10 seconds ago from Twitteratti

...WE'LL MOVE THE PERMANENT STAFF IN NEXT WEEK. TOP CHEFS, FULL MAID SERVICE, THE WORKS. WE'LL DO SOME *VIDEO TOURS* FOR ALL THE BIG CELEBRITY NEWS SHOWS...
CAN WE GET TO THE PART WHERE WE ACTUALLY GET TO BE *SUPER-HEROES?*
HEY.
WHAT'S *THIS* COMING?
THAT'S A LOT OF REFRESHMENT.
SOMEBODY HAVING A *PARTY--?*
NICELY OBSERVED, LANTERN BOY...
...THINK OF IT AS A MASSIVE *COMING OUT* PARTY. FOR YOU GUYS. A "WELCOME TO THE WORLD STAGE" SHINDIG.
Open bar, I hope?
NATURALLY.
WHY DID I LEAVE MY *OWN* TV SHOW IF WE'RE JUST GETTING BACK ON THE SAME TREADMILL? I HAD A KILLER MERCH DEAL...!
THAT WAS THEN. THIS IS NOW.
WHY DO YOU THINK WE PUT YOUR HEADQUARTERS ON AN ORBITING SATELLITE? *FORGET* THE NARROW MARKET THAT SPAWNED YOU. IT'S TIME TO THINK *GLOBALLY*.

@MOSEXSBAT: THIS SHOULD BE MORE THRILLING FOR ME...
about 7 seconds ago from Twitteratti
YOU WANNA SAVE THE *WORLD*, RIGHT?

Our meeting table...
@MOSEXSBAT: I DON'T FEEL MUCH LIKE A PARTY.
about 15 seconds ago from Twitteratti
THIS IS ALL FOR US?
IS THAT OSHIZUSHI?
HOLD ON, TEAM. HAVING OUR MEETINGS CATERED SHOULD BE EXPECTED, BUT AN ICE SCULPTURE IS JUST LAME.
SO, MISTER HANOVER-PUBLICIST, WHO'S SHOWING UP FOR THIS "PARTY"...?
IT IS OSHIZUSHI...!
THE QUESTION IS-- WHO ISN'T SHOWING UP? YOU DID A HELLUVA JOB BRANDING YOURSELVES IN JAPAN, BUT THE REAL CULTURE VULTURES GENERALLY FLY WEST.
BUT, Y'KNOW, FORGET ABOUT EAST-VS-WEST. THE WHOLE PURPOSE OF THIS SATELLITE IS TO PUT SUPER YOUNG TEAM IN A NEW CONTEXT.
THEY TELL ME THIS PLACE WAS ENGINEERED TO SKIP ACROSS THE ATMOSPHERE WITHOUT BURNING UP IN RE-ENTRY...
...TALK ABOUT A VIEW!

@MOSEXSBAT: HIP-HOP/CLASSIC ROCK MASH-UPS ARE SO LAST YEAR.
about 20 seconds ago from Twitteratti
@MOSEXSBAT: THESE CLUBBERS DON'T EVEN HAVE SUPERPOWERS. WORTHLESS.
about 3 seconds ago from Twitteratti
I'VE SEEN SOME OF THESE FACES ON TELEVISION. THEY'RE THE BEST KIND OF FAMOUS...

You mean, famous for doing *nothing?*
Let's see *them* try and to rescue reality...

Bartender, got any Suntory back there?
Don't worry, I'm totally legal. Plus, I'm a superhero.
And wipe that smirk off your face.

--ON THE SCENE FOR *ENTERTAINMENT EXTRA!* THE *STARS* CAME OUT IN FORCE FOR THE OPENING GALA OF THE SUPER YOUNG TEAM'S SATELLITE EXTRAVAGANZA!
THE MUSIC IS *POUNDING* AND THE CROWD IS *LOVING* IT AS THEY RUB ELBOWS WITH JAPAN'S LATEST TEEN IMPORTS!

...I just don't think he *heard* you when all of time and space was shredding under our feet.
HE HEARD ME.
EVERYONE HEARD ME.
Sorry, Kim.
No one takes those kinds of proclamations seriously when the world is burning.
WELL, I BEG TO DIFFER--
WHOA--!
YO! SHINY HAPPY AQUAZON! RIGHT *ON!*
THEY CALL ME *RAZZLE!* I'M ONE OF THE *PROMOTERS* HERE. I BROUGHT DJ JUPITA UP TO ROCK THE MOONBASE!
SO, WHADDYA THINK? ME, I THINK THE TWO OF US ARE ON THE SAME *WAVE-LENGTH* HERE! I CAN GET YOU INTO ANY CLUB WHEN JUPITA'S SET WRAPS...
NO THANKS. TOO MANY PAPARAZZI AROUND THESE DAYS.
HEY-*YO--!*
THERE'S ALWAYS A *BACK ENTRANCE!* YA *FEEL* ME, GIRL?!

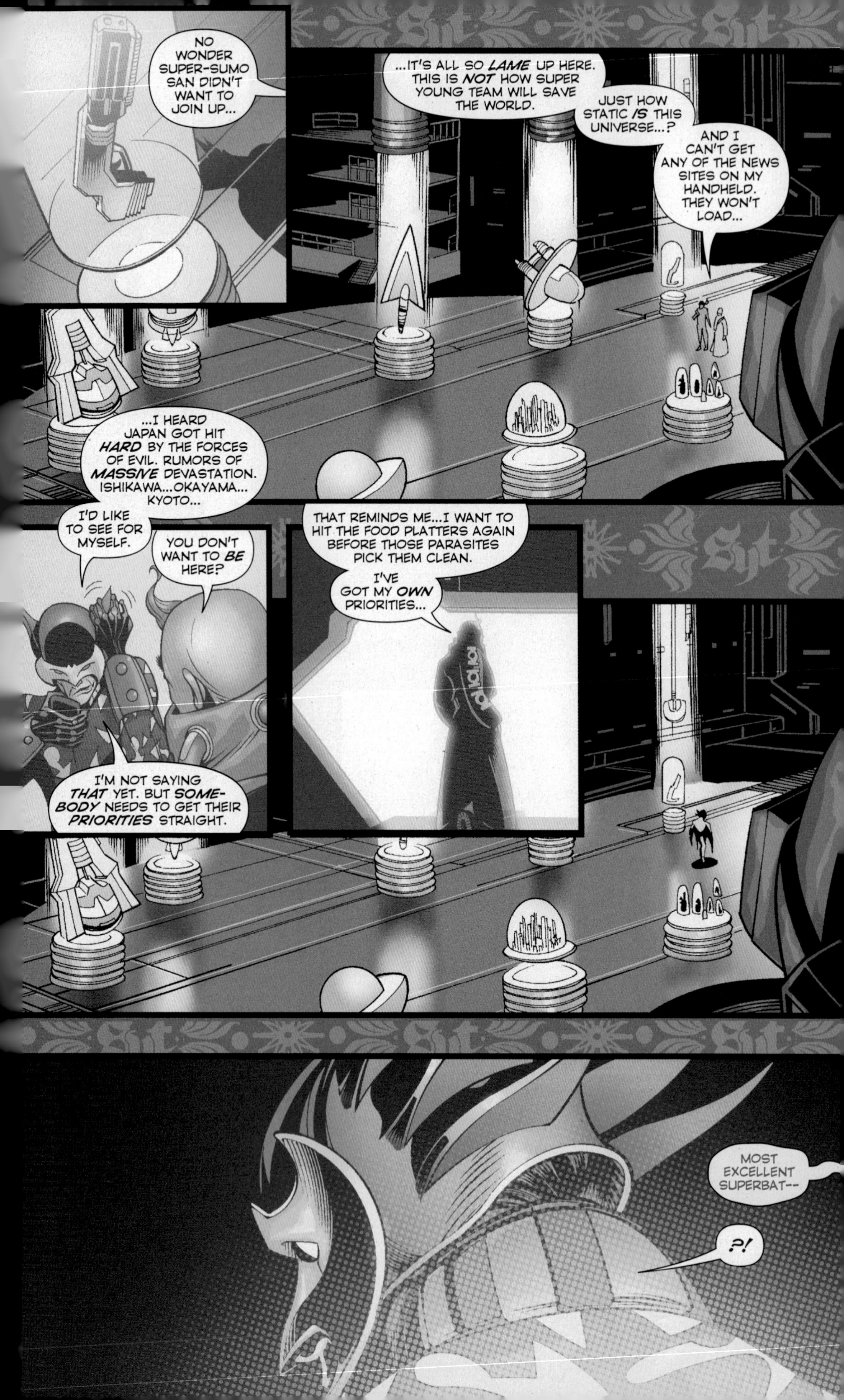
NO WONDER SUPER-SUMO SAN DIDN'T WANT TO JOIN UP...
...IT'S ALL SO LAME UP HERE. THIS IS NOT HOW SUPER YOUNG TEAM WILL SAVE THE WORLD.
JUST HOW STATIC IS THIS UNIVERSE...?
AND I CAN'T GET ANY OF THE NEWS SITES ON MY HANDHELD. THEY WON'T LOAD...
...I HEARD JAPAN GOT HIT HARD BY THE FORCES OF EVIL. RUMORS OF MASSIVE DEVASTATION. ISHIKAWA...OKAYAMA... KYOTO...
I'D LIKE TO SEE FOR MYSELF.
YOU DON'T WANT TO BE HERE?
I'M NOT SAYING THAT YET. BUT SOME-BODY NEEDS TO GET THEIR PRIORITIES STRAIGHT.
THAT REMINDS ME...I WANT TO HIT THE FOOD PLATTERS AGAIN BEFORE THOSE PARASITES PICK THEM CLEAN.
I'VE GOT MY OWN PRIORITIES...
MOST EXCELLENT SUPERBAT--
?!

--STAND PROUDLY OR NOT AT ALL!
EACH AND EVERY HERO IS PART OF SOMETHING GREATER THAN THEMSELVES-- A GRAND TAPESTRY!
THE TRADITIONS YOU MOCK ARE THE SACRIFICES MADE IN YOUR HONOR!
BUT THERE IS STILL HOPE.
YOU... YOU'RE--
--ULTIMON--?!
I AM MORE THAN ULTIMON.
I AM THE ORIGINAL! I AM THE SPIRIT OF THE MASTER MONSTER KILLER!
I AM ULTIMON-ALPHA!
FROM THEIR ATTACK BASE ABOVE MOUNT FUJI, MY FINAL SUCCESSOR AND HIS HERO-TEAM--BIG SCIENCE ACTION--WERE THE PROTECTORS OF OUR ISLAND EMPIRE. THEY WERE AN INSPIRATION!
BUT THAT WAS DECADES AGO. AND EACH GENERATION DEPENDS ON THE NEXT TO ASCEND TO EVEN GREATER GLORIES!

YOU HAVE BEEN IGNORING YOUR *RESPONSIBILITIES!*
ULTIMON-ALPHA. YOU *ARE* THE MAD MONSTA-KILLA, AREN'T YOU...?
CAN I GET A *PICTURE* WITH YOU...?
OPEN YOUR EYES. OBSERVE THE WORLD AROUND YOU, MOST EXCELLENT SUPERBAT.
FIND OUT WHERE YOU ARE MOST NEEDED AND TAKE *IMMEDIATE ACTION*...
@MOSEXSBAT: I DON'T BELIEVE IN GHOSTS.
about 2 seconds ago from Twitteratti

@MOSEXSBAT: BUT I'M ALSO THE SANEST SUPERHERO I KNOW.
about 5 seconds ago from Twitteratti

WHO'S CATERING THIS PARTY? WAY TOO SLOW RE-CIRCULATING THE APPETIZER TRAYS...
Hush, Boy. I'm trying to focus...
...trying to see if there's even still an Earth down there.
--JUST HEAR ME OUT! WE COULD TAKE YOU TO A WHOLE 'NOTHER LEVEL!
AND I'M NOT JUST TALKING ABOUT SEX! WE'D BE LIKE BUSINESS PARTNERS--!
WITH BENEFITS!
ANYONE GOT THEIR CAMERA PHONE WORKING?
NOT THEM--I WAS TALKING ABOUT GETTING PICS OF US. WE LOOK TOTALLY HOT...
WHY BOTHER? I DON'T EVEN KNOW WHO THESE GUYS ARE. I THOUGHT WE'D BE SEEING SUPERMAN OR GREEN LANTERN OR SOMEBODY...!
...NO ONE WANTS THEIR PICTURE...!

BREAKING NEWS, TEAM. THE WORLD JUST OPENED UP TO ME.
NEITHER OF YOU HAVE EXPERIENCED ANY RECENT HALLUCINATIONS, RIGHT...?
I'm waiting to see JAPAN. But it's all going by so FAST...!
INTERESTING. I WAS TRYING TO GET AN UPDATE ON MY--
HEY, HEROES--

--SOME OF YOU AREN'T CIRCULATING LIKE YOU SHOULD BE. A FEW BFF'S OUT OF THIS CROWD AND YOU'LL REACH A WHOLE NEW LEVEL.
ISN'T THIS WHAT YOU WANTED?
You're a little out of DATE, Mister Hanover. That was BEFORE.
We've got a responsibility to our HOME-LAND--
UNDERSTOOD, LITTLE BIRD...

...BUT YOU NEED TO ACCEPT YOUR RESPONSIBILITIES TO THE REST OF THE WORLD. YOU'VE GOT PEOPLE WHO'RE DEEPLY INVESTED IN YOUR PROGRESS.
TRUST ME, JAPAN WILL BE THERE WHEN THE RIDE'S ALL OVER. YOU'VE ONLY GOT ONE CHANCE TO MAKE A FIRST IMPRESSION.
THAT'S AMERICA DOWN THERE, BABY...
...THEY NEED NEW HEROES, TOO.
@MOSEXSBAT: LAND OF THE FREE ENTERPRISE. HOME OF THE NO-INTEREST LOAN. about 7 seconds ago from Twitteratti

MIDWAY CITY:
RECON SEVEN, HAVE YOU REACHED THE TARGET AREA? OVER...
ROGER THAT, CENTER. I'M PASSING OVER DOWNTOWN MIDWAY RIGHT NOW. SENSORS ARE ACTIVE...
...PICKING UP SOME NOMINAL BACKGROUND RADIATION. SHALL I SET HER DOWN AND GET A CLOSER LOOK? OVER...
THAT'S A BIG NEGATIVE, SEVEN. WE JUST GOT THE WORD THAT MIDWAY CITY IS QUARANTINED. JLA-APPROVED RESCUE WORKERS ONLY ON THE GROUND. OVER...
ROGER THAT. ANY IDEA WHEN THAT'LL BE? EVEN FROM THIS ALTITUDE... IT LOOKS PRETTY HAIRY DOWN THERE...
...DOES ANYONE KNOW FOR SURE WHAT HAPPENED HERE? OVER...
WE DON'T ASK THOSE QUESTIONS, SEVEN. NEITHER SHOULD YOU. JUST GET YOUR SENSOR READINGS AND BRING IT ON IN. OVER...
OBEY
KSEID
NO LIFE WITHOUT ANTI-LIFE
COPY THAT, CENTER...
...I'M COMING HOME.
LET'S HOPE THE RESCUE WORKERS CAN FIND SOMETHING WORTHWHILE IN THIS HELLHOLE.
Y'KNOW, I HAD AN EX WHO LIVED IN A MIDWAY SUBURB. NICE GIRL.
@MOSEXSBAT: FOLLOWING THE RULES IS AS PASSÉ AS PASSÉ GETS.
about 4 seconds ago from Twitteratti

@MOSEXSBAT: SUPERHEROES ARE THE ONLY PURE ORIGINALS LEFT.
about 10 seconds ago from Twitteratti
THE JUSTICE LEAGUE NEVER HOSTED AN OPEN HOUSE. AND THEY'RE YESTERDAY'S HEROES.
NOTHING ABOUT THIS SPEAKS TO OUR TRUE NATURE...
I SAY WE HOP THE TUBE AND HIT HARAJUKU HARD. LIKE WE USED TO.
I AGREE WITH HALF OF YOUR SENTIMENT, LIGHTNING FLASH.
IT'S THE "LIKE WE USED TO" BIT THAT DOESN'T SIT WELL.
THIS IS AN OUTRAGE--
--THE SHAME OF OUR HOME-LAND--

--WHAT DRAGONS HAVE THEY SLAIN?! WHAT TORTUROUS BEASTS HAVE THEY VANQUISHED?!
THIS RIDICULOUS FARCE! THIS UNGRATEFUL PARADE!
WHERE IS YOUR NOBILITY, YOUNG SIRES?! YOU ARE A DISGRACE TO ALL THOSE WHO PRECEDED YOU!
EVEN NOW, YOU MOCK ME! I AM RISING SUN--!
I WILL NOT BE--
WHA--?!
YOU DARE LAY HANDS ON ME?!
SECURITY
YOU NEED TO COME WITH US, SIR...

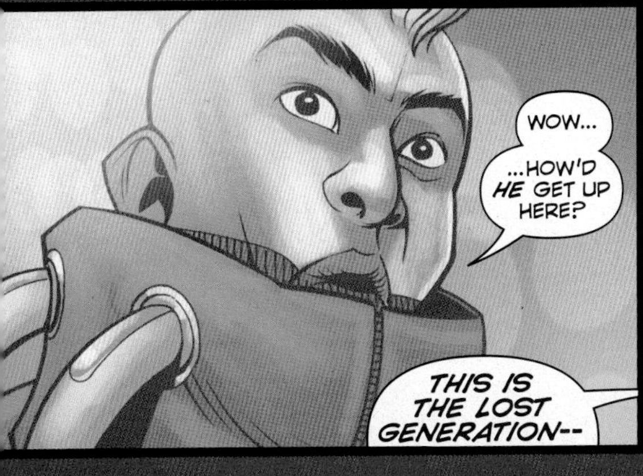
WOW...
...HOW'D HE GET UP HERE?
THIS IS THE LOST GENERATION--

YIKES. SOMEONE NEEDS TO HIT THE STAIRMASTER...
NO DOUBT.

--THE WORLD CANNOT RECOVER!
CAN YOU COMPREHEND?! THERE ARE NEW MONSTERS AT OUR DOOR-STEP!

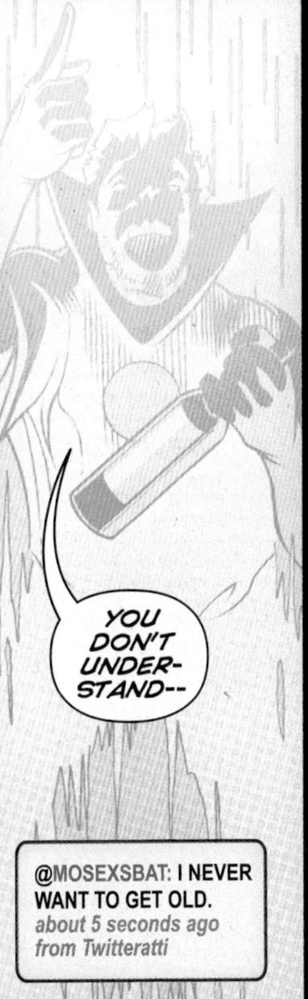
YOU DON'T UNDER-STAND--
@MOSEXSBAT: I NEVER WANT TO GET OLD.
about 5 seconds ago from Twitteratti

OKAY, HOLD UP. LEMME MAKE ONE LAST PITCH...
PERSONALLY, I THINK THE WHOLE ANIME/ MANGA THING IS OVER, BUT YOU'RE BIGGER THAN THAT. I CAN GET YOU PAST THE--
YOU AMERICANS--
--HEY!
SCUMBAG! GET IT STRAIGHT BEFORE I'M FORCED TO DROWN YOU--
--YOU ARE OUT OF MY LEAGUE! SO GET OVER YOURSELF!
Y-YOU...
...YOU'RE JUDGING ME?!
NOBODY KEEPS ME BEHIND THE ROPE, HONEY! NOBODY KEEPS ME OUT OF THE CLUB! OR THEIR PANTS!
NOBODY!
HEINO! THIS PARTY JUST GOT INTERESTING!
LOOK--!
NOBODY... TURNS ME DOWN!
I'M
RAAAZZLLEE--!
AND I WANT YOOOUUU--!

@MOSEXSBAT: MONSTER-PROMOTER. YOU TAKE WHAT YOU CAN GET.
about 1 second ago from Twitteratti
ANOTHER CALL TO ACTION!
MISSION-STATEMENT:-SAVESHINY-HAPPY-AQUAZON--!
YOU THINK I'M JUST A FETISH?!
I'M ALL ABOUT UNDERWATER MUNITIONS!
GET AWAY FROM HER!
HEY--
--I HAD HIM IN MY SIGHTS...!

I'M WHAT'S HAPPENING!
I'M THE DATE-RAPE POSTER BOY--!
I don't doubt it, Busu--
SUMMIMASSENNN!!
@MOSEXSBAT: SOME MOVES FEEL BETTER THAN OTHERS.
about 1 femtosecond ago from Twitteratti
DAMMIT!
YOU COMPLETELY LEFT ME OUT OF YOUR SUPER TEAM-WORK--!

H-HEY! NICE BIT OF B-ROLL THERE, EH...?
OH, SHE BLEW OUT YOUR EQUIPMENT, DIDN'T SHE...?
LET ME HELP YOU TO--
TOO LITTLE, TOO LATE, LANTERN--
--DON'T TOUCH ME!
THAT WAS QUICK.
Can we drag the carcass into our trophy room...?
DON'T FORGET... THAT'S NOT OUR TROPHY ROOM, LOLITA CANARY.
SOMEONE ELSE PAID FOR IT.
@MOSEXSBAT: OUR LIFE HAS TO BE MORE THAN A SOUND BYTE.
about 4 seconds ago from Twitteratti
innovative concepts
I'D HAVE TO SAY THAT HANOVER IS DOING HIS JOB QUITE WELL, UNDER THE CIRCUMSTANCES...
@MOSEXSBAT: WHO CLOCKS THE CLOCKMEN?
about 2 seconds ago from Twitteratti
pOpTEEN
SUPER YOUNG TEAM!
THE TRUTH BEHIND SUPERBAT'S TV SHOW!
THEY'RE EXACTLY WHAT YOU WANT!
THE NEW FASHION WHAT THEY'RE WEARING THIS WEEK ON THE
SHINY HAPPY AQUAZON WHAT HER FATHER
BIG LANTERN BOY INTERVIEW

...NO ONE COULD'VE PREDICTED THAT MUTANT PROMOTER. THAT WAS AN UNFORTUNATE VARIABLE.
IT WAS SLOPPY! THERE WAS A LACK OF ATTENTION TO DETAIL!
WE HIRED YOU TO USE THESE FALSE IDOLS TO DISTRACT THE WORLD FROM THE CURRENT PLIGHT OF OUR HOMELAND!
DUE RESPECT, MISTER ITAMI...BUT THE SATELLITE IS MERELY PHASE ONE. PART OF A SIX-POINT PLAN...
BESIDES, IT'S OUR UNDERSTANDING THAT THESE KIDS HAVE NO INTEREST IN TRYING TO "SAVE" ANYTHING! THEY'RE NOT HEROES IN THE TRADITIONAL SENSE...
THAT REMAINS TO BE SEEN, GENTLEMEN. THEY HAVE THEIR OWN BRAND OF AMBITION... WHICH MAKES THEM VERY DANGEROUS.
THE WORLD MUST NEVER KNOW THE TRUTH ABOUT JAPAN. EVEN OUR OWN CITIZENS MUST NOT KNOW.
WE ARE COUNTING ON YOUR ORGANIZATION TO ENSURE THIS OBFUSCATION.
DO WHAT MUST BE DONE.
NEXT DANCE MOVE:
OXYGEN

CHAPTER TWO

André Coelho & Eduardo Pansica ▮ Pencillers
André Coelho & Sandro Ribeiro ▮ Inkers

BISHŌJO RISING
LAS VULGAR!
WHAT HAPPENS HERE--STAYS HERE!
LIVE SHOW
JESUS
PLAY

@MOSEXSBAT: AMERICA WEARS ITS SOUL ON ITS FACE. WELL-INTENTIONED BUT MISGUIDED.
about 1 minute ago from Twitteratti
I FEEL YOU. SERIOUSLY. EVERYBODY AND THEIR MOTHER HAS A SATELLITE HEADQUARTERS. TOTAL CLICHÉ...
...THIS IS MORE YOUR SPEED, I'LL BET.
THEY'VE ALREADY RENAMED IT THE SUPER YOUNG TEAM SUITE. THE VERY DEFINITION OF SWANK, BELIEVE ME.
WE'VE GOT A FILM CREW READY TO GET IT ALL ON VIDEO. THEY'RE THE BEST IN THE BUSINESS...
... THEY'LL DOCUMENT YOUR RISE TO UBIQUITY. A LITTLE CREATIVE EDITING, AND YOU'LL COME ACROSS AS MYTHIC.
SO, C'MON, TAKE A LOOK AROUND.
I ALREADY DID. SAW ALL THE ROOMS. JUST NOW.
NOT BAD. SEEN BETTER.
I'M WITH WELL-SPOKEN SONIC LIGHTNING FLASH.
IT'S NO CLASKA.
The bar is fully stocked,

AND FULLY COMPED. PLUS, THERE'S A HOT TUB OUT ON THE BALCONY. Y'KNOW, IN CASE ANY OF YOU ARE FEELING...AMOROUS TOWARD EACH OTHER.
SEX SELLS.
WELL...
SO DOES TURNING STARRO INTO SUSHI OR CAUSING MANDRAKK TO WET HIMSELF.
I CAN'T FAKE WHAT ISN'T THERE.
DENIED.
YET AGAIN.
WHYS
Photo ops and alcohol don't mix.
This is serious.
JUST DO WHAT YOU DO. PRETEND LIKE THEY AREN'T EVEN HERE.
OH! I'VE ALSO LINED UP A FEW PRODUCT ENDORSEMENTS TO GET YOU OUT IN THE ADVERTISING ARENA.
YOU WANT WORLDWIDE RECOGNITION? THE SHORTEST DISTANCE BETWEEN TWO POINTS IS--
HANOVER--
--YOU'RE TOO FAR INSIDE THE BOX. WE'RE SUPER-HEROES.
AND, AS SUPERHEROES, WE'RE ABOVE ENDORSEMENTS. WE'RE ABOVE ALL THE OLD PARADIGMS.
IF YOU WOULD JUST FOLLOW OUR LEAD AND LET US--
I'LL DO IT...
...BRING ON THE PRODUCT PLACEMENT.
BRAND ME, BABY.

KIM... WHAT ARE YOU SAYING?
YOU CAN'T ALLOW YOURSELF TO BE--
EXPLOITED? YOU THINK I CAN'T HANDLE MYSELF?
@MOSEXSBAT: APPARENTLY, I HAVE A TEAMMATE THAT IS ACTING OUT.
about 2 seconds ago from Twitteratti
SHINY HAPPY AQUAZON. HEY, I'LL TAKE WHAT I CAN GET.
GOT A BIG MEETING LINED UP FOR THIS AFTERNOON. HUGE CAMPAIGN. YOU'RE GOING TO LOVE WHAT--
SO THIS IS HOW YOU DEFINE "SWANK," MISTER HANOVER...
...TWELVE HUNDRED CHANNELS ON THIS THING, BUT NO NEWS STATIONS?
WAIT. NO GBS? NO SUN TV? NO BBC EVEN?
MAYBE THEY DON'T WANT THEIR GAMBLERS DISTRACTED BY THE STATE OF THE OUTSIDE WORLD...
...LAS VULGAR IS ITS OWN POCKET UNIVERSE.
THIS GENERATION, THEY BARELY QUESTION THEIR ENVIRONMENT. AS LONG AS THEIR PLEASURE CENTERS ARE BEING ADEQUATELY STIMULATED.
THEY'RE JUST KIDS...
...GETTING THEM ON TV IS A GOOD BET. ONE SEASON AND THEY WON'T BE ABLE TO DISCERN REALITY...!
EXACTLY WHAT MISTER ITAMI AND HIS BACKERS WANT. ANYTHING TO KEEP THE FOCUS ON THEM AND NOT ON THEIR HOMELAND.
IF YOU SAY SO.
ANYONE KNOW WHAT IS HAPPENING IN JAPAN...?

THE DISRESPECT ON DISPLAY BEFORE ME!
SUCH BLATANT DISREGARD FOR YOUR SACRED HISTORY!
WELCOME TO TOKYO
LET ME PASS, SOLDIER!
APOLOGIES, BUT TOKYO IS QUARANTINED.
QUARANTINED?! I AM RISING SUN! I REPRESENT THE LEGACY OF BIG SCIENCE ACTION! I WAS A MEMBER OF THE GLOBAL GUARDIANS!
AGAIN, APOLOGIES.
HOW DARE YOU?!
IS THE FOLLY OF YOUR ACTIONS COMPLETELY LOST ON YOU?!
WE ARE CHARGED WITH GUARDING OUR CITIES BY LAND, BY AIR AND BY SEA. NO ONE IN OR OUT.
TOYKO IS OFF-LIMITS. EVEN TO YOU, HONORED SUN.

INSOLENT WHELPS! CALL ME RISING SUN!
SHALL I SHOW YOU WHY?!
ONCE AGAIN, APOLOGIES. BUT WE HAVE OUR ORDERS.
YOU DARE TRAIN YOUR WEAPONS ON ME?!
MUST I DEMONSTRATE THE FIRE THAT FELLED A THOUSAND MONSTERS?!
LET YOUR FAMILIES PRAY FOR YOUR--
THAT'S ENOUGH, YASUNARI-SAN...
...THIS IS NO LONGER THE HOMELAND YOU REMEMBER. WE HAVE EXPERIENCED A CRISIS, AND YOU NO LONGER HAVE THE SKILLS TO AID US IN OUR RECOVERY.
YOU KNOW ME. YOU KNOW MY ASSOCIATES. DO NOT TEST US...
...FOR YOU WILL LOSE.
I DO KNOW YOU, ITAMI! I KNOW WHAT YOU AND YOURS REPRESENT!
THIS IS TRULY A DAY OF SHAME WHEN JAPAN TURNS ITS HEROES AWAY!
INDEED. BUT THE SHAME IS YOURS, YASUNARI-SAN.
YOURS AND ALL THOSE WHO WEAR YOUR COLORS.

THIS LIFESTYLE HOLDS NO MEANING...
WHY DO YOU FILM US WHEN WE DO NOTHING...?
NEVER MIND THEM. I'VE BEEN CROSS-REFERENCING LAS VULGAR ON META-WIKI--
--AND I JUST PINGED SOMEONE!
DO YOU KNOW WHO LIVES HERE?
SORRY. WHO'S "DOC DREAD"?
@MOSEXSBAT: PILOTING THE WONDER WAGON TO MEET A BONA FIDE SUPERVILLAIN.
about 5 minutes ago from Twitteratti
WIKI SAYS HE WAS A CRIMINAL MASTERMIND BACK IN THE DAY. WAGED A FULL-ON "WAR AGAINST SOCIETY"...
...THAT'S GOOD ENOUGH FOR ME.
SAYS HERE HE LAID LOW AFTER HIS GANG WAS INFILTRATED BY METAMORPHO, THE ELEMENT MAN. A JUSTICE LEAGUER!
What about the camera crew?
FOR THE NEXT FIVE HOURS...
"... THEY WILL BE OTHERWISE OCCUPIED."
@MOSEXSBAT: I'M WAY TOO RICH TO BE ON AMERICAN TELEVISION.
about 1 minute ago from Twitteratti

HHHSSSSS...
OXYGEN
KAFF KOFF AHUH--
WHU-WHAT *IS* THIS SUBSTANCE--?!
PURE OXYGEN. WITH A FEW *BOOSTER* ENHANCEMENTS, I'D IMAGINE. NOW DO ME A FAVOR, AQUAZON...
...THIS IS THE *PRESIDENT* OF OXY-GEN, INC. MISTER *COREY WELBOURNE.*
SO POSITIVELY THRILLED YOU'VE AGREED TO WORK WITH US.
THIS IS A MATCH MADE IN HEAVEN. A NEW-GEN *SUPERHERO* ENDORSING THE NEXT-GEN IN *REFRESHMENT*.
OXY-GEN IS THE *BEST* OF WHAT WE NEED TO BREATHE.
HERE, IF YOU'LL ALLOW ME...
HHHSSSSS...
SO...INCREDIBLY... INVIGORATING...
UMMM... RIGHT. WELL...
WE ALL KNOW THAT, IN THIS DAY AND AGE, IT PAYS TO MOVE *QUICKLY*...
...LET'S STRIKE BEFORE THIS WHOLE THING IS SEEN AS JUST ANOTHER *FAD*.
HMMM...

@MOSEXSBAT: DOC DREAD HAS A WELCOMING COMMITTEE. I LIKE HIM ALREADY.
about 6 minutes ago from Twitteratti
TWELVE MORE SECONDS AND I'M GOING TO BLOW YOUR MINDS.
AS YOU CAN SEE, WE'VE GOT THE BEST GRAPHIC DESIGNERS AT OUR DISPOSAL...
...AND, VOILA. THE CAMPAIGN IN ALL ITS ITERATIONS. WORLD PENETRATION THROUGH VISUALS.
HOW 'BOUT THAT, AQUAZON? THIS COULDN'T HAVE WORKED OUT BETTER.
YOU'LL BOTH BE HOUSEHOLD NAMES BEFORE THE END OF THE WEEK.
DO I HAVE LIKENESS APPROVAL?

ARE YOU KIDDING? HOW MUCH CLOSER COULD THEY GET?!
UNLESS YOU WANT US TO SHAVE OFF SOME CELLULITE OR BRING YOU UP A CUP SIZE OR TWO...
WELL...
HHHSSSSS...
TRUST ME, YOU AND OUR PRODUCT ARE EQUALLY SEDUCTIVE. YOURS IS VISUAL. OURS IS...SPIRITUAL.
ONCE YOU'VE BREATHED OXY-GEN, YOU BECOME PART OF SOMETHING MUCH LARGER THAN YOURSELF...
OXY-GEN
Now this is a gamble!
ALLOW ME A CLEAR SHOT--!
@MOSEXSBAT: THIS IS ALL SO MUCH BETTER THAN I'D ANTICIPATED.
about 3 minutes ago from Twitteratti

OKAY, SO...WE'RE GOING TO USE THIS LIVE EVENT TO LAUNCH THIS P.R. BONANZA. THE PRESS IS HERE...THE PUBLIC'S HERE...IT'S A HAPPENING.
THIS IS JUST THE FIRST STEP OF A WORLDWIDE CAMPAIGN--OXY-GEN FOR EVERYONE! SHOULD BE A REAL BLAST!
OXY
BULLSEYE!
WAITAMINUTE! WAITAMINUTE! DON'T--!
YOU KIDS ARE THE ONES TRESPASSING! THIS IS MY TURF! YOU THINK I'M NOT GONNA PROTECT IT?!
NOT THE FACE! NOT THE FACE!

COMMERCIALISM. CAPITALISM. SHOW BUSINESS.
SHOULDN'T I DEMONSTRATE MY TALENTS IN SOME WAY? DID YOU HIRE A SUPERVILLAIN FOR ME TO FIGHT?
THIS IS JUST A GRIP-AND-GRIN. LET WELBOURNE DO HIS THING. YOU JUST WAVE AND SMILE...
FOLKS, THANKS SO MUCH FOR BEING HERE! I CAN ALREADY TELL YOU'RE ALL STARVED FOR A NEW KIND OF REFRESHMENT!
OXY-GEN-- IN PARTNERSHIP WITH THE DEVONSHIRE CORPORATION AND TECHNOCULT--NOT ONLY BRINGS YOU A BURST OF FRESHNESS YOU CAN CARRY WITH YOU...
...WE'RE BRINGING YOU OUR VERY OWN SUPERHERO! FROM THE WORLD RENOWNED SUPER YOUNG TEAM, SAY HELLO TO SHINY HAPPY AQUAZON!
...HONESTLY, I THOUGHT THIS WAS SOME SORT OF SETUP. FIGURED YOU'D BROUGHT A CAMERA CREW WITH YOU.
WELL, NO.
THEN AGAIN, NO ONE'S REALLY HEARD OF ME, EITHER.
BUT, DOC, WE SAVED THE MULTIVERSE!
KID, THAT PARTICULAR FEAT IS ON, JUST ABOUT EVERY HERO'S RÉSUMÉ. I JUST DON'T WANT TO BE CAST AS ANYONE'S TV NEMESIS...
SO YOU'VE HEARD OF US?
DUE RESPECT, DOCTOR, BUT WE AIM TO DO THINGS OUR WAY! WE'RE OUT TO CULTIVATE OUR OWN ARCHENEMIES. WE ARE THE FUTURE OF THE SUPER-LIFESTYLE CHOICE!
CALM DOWN. WE ARE GUESTS HERE.
NO, I GET IT. BELIEVE ME, I'VE BEEN THERE.
I WANTED TO MAKE A NAME FOR MYSELF, TOO.
YOU'D BE SURPRISED AT WHAT IT TAKES TO BE ORIGINAL IN THIS GAME.

WE'VE DISTRIBUTED FREE SAMPLES OF OUR PRODUCT TO EACH AND EVERY ONE OF YOU!
THE ENTIRE WORLD WILL SOON EXPERIENCE! SO TAKE YOUR PATENTED OXY-GEN DELIVERY CANISTERS, PLACE THEM TO YOUR AIRWAYS--
--AND LET US ALL BECOME ONE.
OXY-GEN
"... ALL BECOME ONE"?! DID THIS JUST MORPH INTO SOCIALISM?
YOU HAVE ACTED OF YOUR OWN ACCORD--
--AND YOU HAVE SURRENDERED ALL FREE WILL TO THE COLLECTIVE CONCEPT!
I AM NOW WITHIN EACH OF YOU! YOU ARE NOW EXTENSIONS OF WHAT I AM!
NOW GO FORTH AND DELIVER MY SINGLE-MINDED SERMON OF DESTRUCTION! YOU HAVE BECOME ONE WITH--
--THE BRAIN DRAIN!

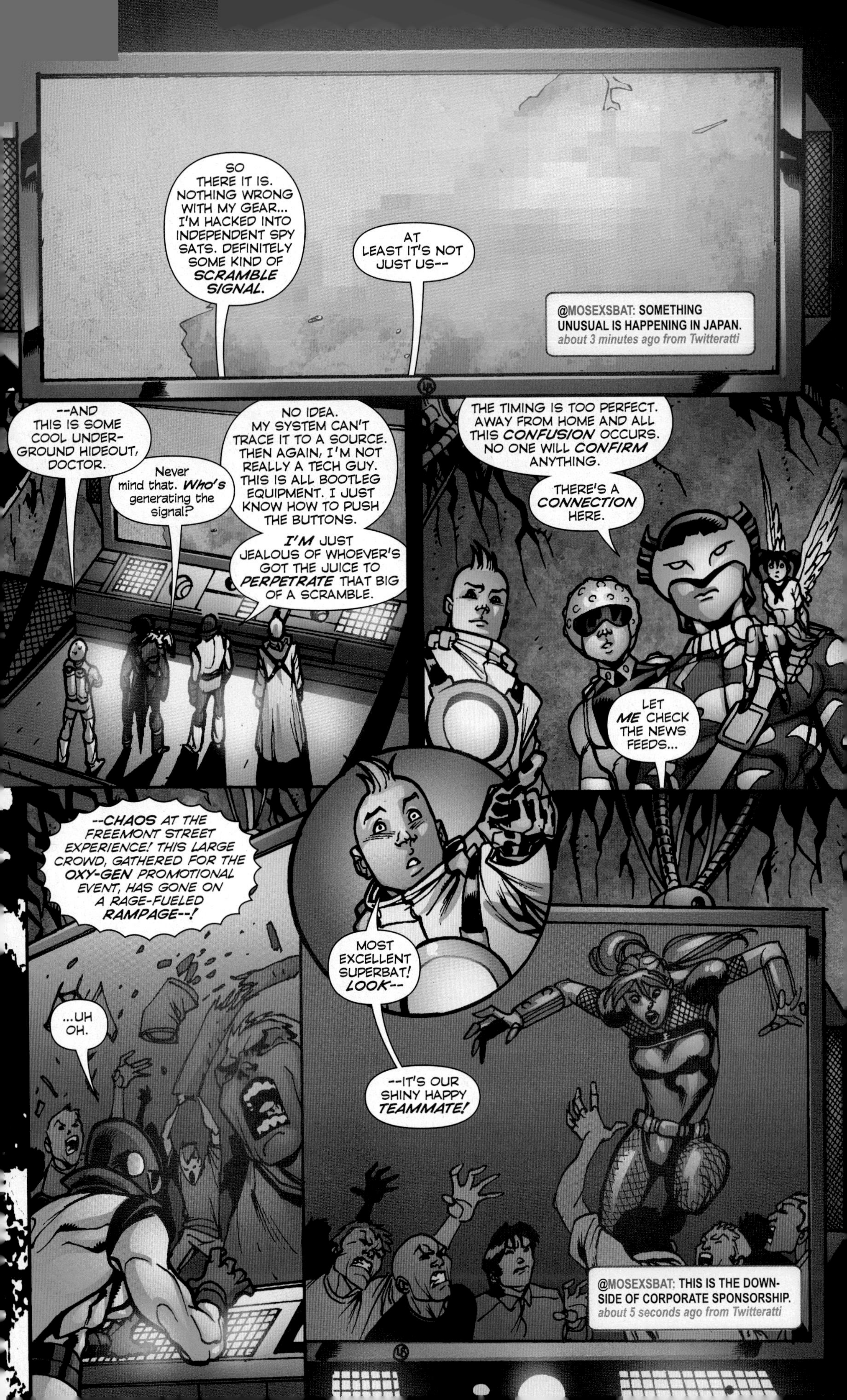

SO THERE IT IS. NOTHING WRONG WITH MY GEAR... I'M HACKED INTO INDEPENDENT SPY SATS. DEFINITELY SOME KIND OF SCRAMBLE SIGNAL.
AT LEAST IT'S NOT JUST US--
@MOSEXSBAT: SOMETHING UNUSUAL IS HAPPENING IN JAPAN.
about 3 minutes ago from Twitteratti
--AND THIS IS SOME COOL UNDER-GROUND HIDEOUT, DOCTOR.
Never mind that. Who's generating the signal?
NO IDEA. MY SYSTEM CAN'T TRACE IT TO A SOURCE. THEN AGAIN, I'M NOT REALLY A TECH GUY. THIS IS ALL BOOTLEG EQUIPMENT. I JUST KNOW HOW TO PUSH THE BUTTONS.
I'M JUST JEALOUS OF WHOEVER'S GOT THE JUICE TO PERPETRATE THAT BIG OF A SCRAMBLE.
THE TIMING IS TOO PERFECT. AWAY FROM HOME AND ALL THIS CONFUSION OCCURS. NO ONE WILL CONFIRM ANYTHING.
THERE'S A CONNECTION HERE.
LET ME CHECK THE NEWS FEEDS...
--CHAOS AT THE FREEMONT STREET EXPERIENCE! THIS LARGE CROWD, GATHERED FOR THE OXY-GEN PROMOTIONAL EVENT, HAS GONE ON A RAGE-FUELED RAMPAGE--!
MOST EXCELLENT SUPERBAT! LOOK--
...UH OH.
--IT'S OUR SHINY HAPPY TEAMMATE!
@MOSEXSBAT: THIS IS THE DOWN-SIDE OF CORPORATE SPONSORSHIP.
about 5 seconds ago from Twitteratti

THE BRAIN DRAIN MAKES YOUR EXISTENCE EASIER!
TOO GOOD TO BE TRUE--
WELBOURNE--!
WHAT HAVE YOU DONE?! WHAT'S THE INGREDIENT IN OXY-GEN THAT CAUSES THIS?!
@MOSEXSBAT: THIS IS HOW A REAL SUPERHERO MAKES AN ENTRANCE.
about 2 seconds ago from Twitteratti

SO OXY-GEN CAUSES SOME KIND OF MOB MENTALITY IN ALL THOSE WHO INHALE IT. BUT TO WHAT END...?
Does everything need a reason?
THAT'S AN EXISTENTIAL QUESTION, CANARY. SAVE IT FOR THE CAMERAS.
I MANAGED TO GRAB A CANISTER. CAN'T... MAKE OUT THE SMALL PRINT...
I know glasses aren't stylish, Kim. But think about it.
No ingredient list. Subsidiary of Devonshire, blah, blah, blah. Wait, here's a location: Oxy-Gen bottling plant...
...Thornton, Colorado.
FAREWELL, LAS VULGAR.
@MOSEXSBAT: NEW ARCHITECTURAL CLASSIFICATION: INDUSTRIAL MYSTERIOSO.
about 2 minutes ago from Twitteratti
I'M OFFICIALLY CREEPED OUT...

...THERE'S NOBODY HERE.
MY EYES ARE FASTER THAN MY FEET. SHE'S RIGHT. THE WHOLE PLANT IS DESERTED.
WHY ARE WE WHISPERING?
WHOA--!
NO! IT'S A TRAP! SCRAMBLE, TEAM!
CHILL OUT, BOY. THIS PLANT IS FULLY AUTO-MATED.
PRODUCING ALL THE OXY-GEN YOU CAN HUFF, TWENTY-FOUR/SEVEN.
And THERE'S where it's all coming from.
Not exactly a Doc Dread, but beggars can't be choosers.
THINKWE'VE ALREADYWONON STYLEPOINTS--
LIGHTNING FLASH--
--WAIT!

SMOOTH.
OF COURSE, IT'S PROTECTED BY A LOCALIZED FORCE FIELD. THAT'S STANDARD VILLAIN PROTOCOL. BUT IT'S MERELY *ENERGY*.
ATOMIC LANTERN BOY.
ADJUST YOUR CHEST BEAMER TO COUNTERACT THE FREQUENCY. JUST TO MAKE A HOLE FOR US.
IT'S ALL INSTINCT--
--*GO!*
KEEP IT TIGHT, KIDDIES.
@MOSEXSBAT: MAYBE NOW WE CAN MAKE A DIFFERENCE.
about 1 second ago from Twitteratti

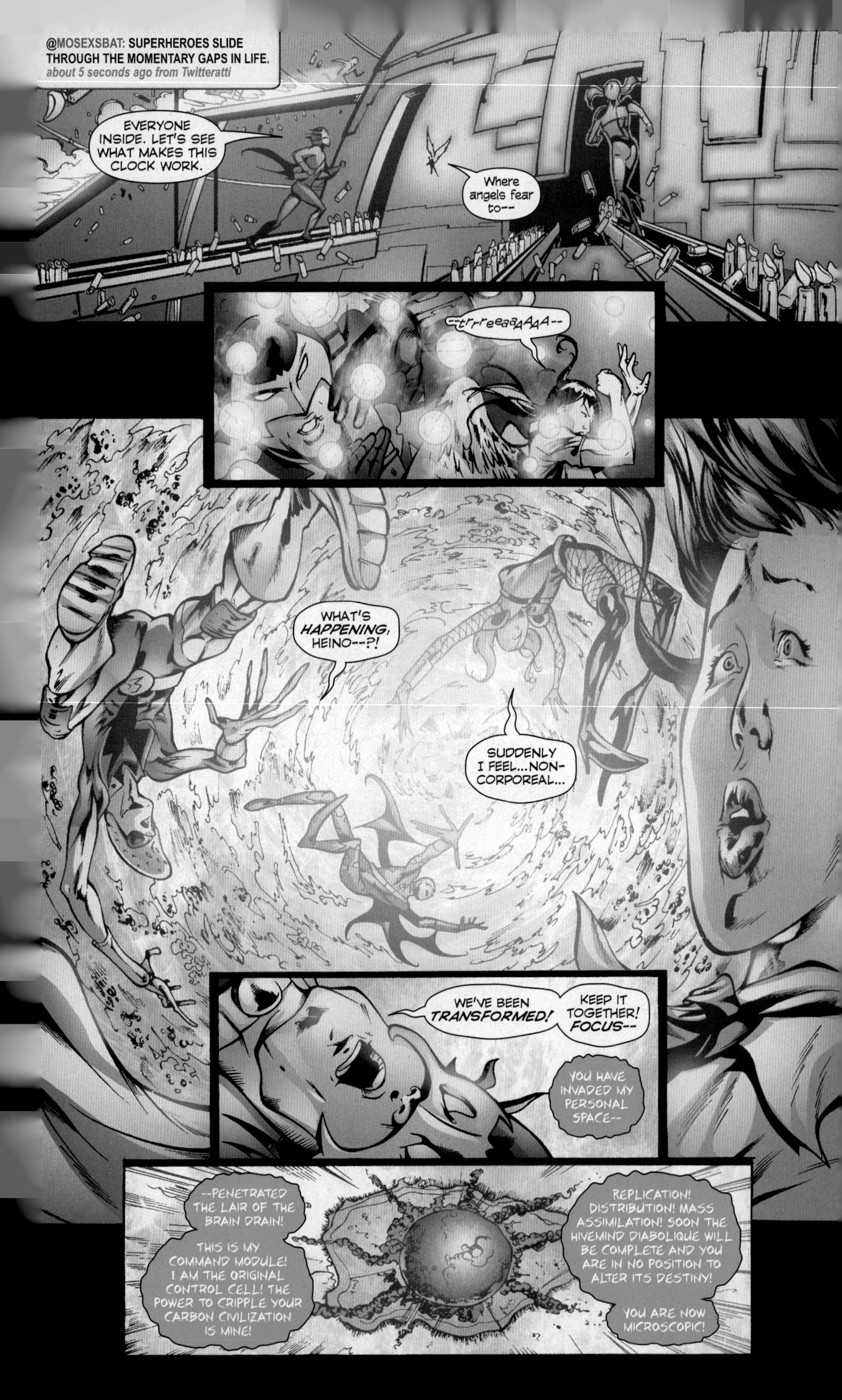
@MOSEXSBAT: SUPERHEROES SLIDE THROUGH THE MOMENTARY GAPS IN LIFE.
about 5 seconds ago from Twitteratti
EVERYONE INSIDE. LET'S SEE WHAT MAKES THIS CLOCK WORK.
Where angels fear to--
--trrreeaaAAAA--
WHAT'S HAPPENING, HEINO--?!
SUDDENLY I FEEL...NON-CORPOREAL...
WE'VE BEEN TRANSFORMED!
KEEP IT TOGETHER! FOCUS--
YOU HAVE INVADED MY PERSONAL SPACE--
--PENETRATED THE LAIR OF THE BRAIN DRAIN!
THIS IS MY COMMAND MODULE! I AM THE ORIGINAL CONTROL CELL! THE POWER TO CRIPPLE YOUR CARBON CIVILIZATION IS MINE!
REPLICATION! DISTRIBUTION! MASS ASSIMILATION! SOON THE HIVEMIND DIABOLIQUE WILL BE COMPLETE AND YOU ARE IN NO POSITION TO ALTER ITS DESTINY!
YOU ARE NOW MICROSCOPIC!

BORED ONCE AGAIN. AND ALL ALONE.
I'M PART OF THIS TEAM. I'M A FOUNDING MEMBER. I SHOULD BE DOING SOMETHING...
...PROACTIVE...?
I AM A SINGLE CELL OF PURE DARK THOUGHT BACTERIA! YOU CANNOT POSSIBLY CHALLENGE ME--
I HOLD IN MY HANDS-- THE SMALLEST SUPERVILLAIN OF ALL!
MICRO-TELEPATHIC ATTACK--!
GYAAAH--!
HNGGG--!
MAYBE I CAN USE SOME SORT OF SUPER-SCIENCE TO ALTER THE OXY-GEN FORMULA TO MAKE EVERYONE...
...LOVE ME.
CANARY! SONIC COUNTER-ATTACK!
ing

SUMMMMMMMMMM
SENNNN!!
MY PLASMA MEMBRANE IS WEAKENED--CYTOPLASM LEAKING--YOU CANNOT--
NOOOOOO OOOOO--
GYUUUHHHNN--!
NNNNNN...
DID... SOMETHING *UNUSUAL* HAPPEN...?
NOTHING TOO COMPLEX. FORCED BINARY FISSION VIA SONIC DEATH WAIL.
BRAIN DRAIN IS NOW JUST ANOTHER ELEMENT OF AMERICAN AIR POLLUTION.
@MOSEXSBAT: STRIKE A POSE WHEN YOU SAVE THE DAY. BRING ON THE GLORY...
about 7 seconds ahead from Twitteratti

...WITH THE COMPLETE RECALL OF ALL OXY-GEN BRAND PRODUCTS FROM STORE SHELVES WORLDWIDE. NO SPECIFIC REASON WAS CITED BY THE COMPANY.
BUT THEY CLAIM THE INCIDENT IN NEVADA HAD NO BEARING ON THEIR ACTIONS...
HOW LONG YOU GONNA NURSE THAT BOTTLE...?
NONE OF YOUR BUSINESS.
HUH. THEM WORMS USUALLY SHOW UP IN MEZCAL. NEVER HEARD OF THIS BRAND. Y'KNOW, EATIN' THE WORM'S SUPPOSED T'GIVE YOU VISIONS...
GLUB
IN THAT CASE...
SATISFIED...?
HIC
NOW LET'S SEE WHAT THE WORM SHOWS ME...
NEXT DANCE MOVE:

CHAPTER THREE

ChrisCross ▮ Penciller
Rob Stull ▮ Inker

@MOSEXSBAT: I'M SO TURNED ON RIGHT NOW.
about 2 seconds ago from Twitteratti

Love Went Mad
THEY MADE IT TO DUBAI...?
JUST GOT WORD...

...TOUCHDOWN IN THE SPANKING NEW DUBAI ENTERTAINMENT CITY. THE HANOVER KID'S ALREADY THERE, READY TO MAKE LEMONADE.
IT'LL BE MEDIA OVERLOAD, NO DOUBT ABOUT IT. NOT TO MENTION, WE'VE GOT OUR INDEPENDENT CONTRACTORS ONSITE, READY FOR THEIR ORDERS.
HOLD IT. CHECK OUT THE NEWS...
--RANDOM FLAME PATTERNS SEEN OVER THE PACIFIC. METEOROLOGISTS AREN'T RULING OUT METAHUMAN ACTIVITY.
IF THAT'S WHO I THINK IT IS...
...THAT COULD ACTUALLY BE USEFUL.
THE JAPANESE ARE SO WORRIED ABOUT NORTH KOREAN META-PROGRAMS, THEY'RE IGNORING THEIR OWN PROBLEM AREAS.
BETTER FOR OUR BUSINESS--
PANT GASP
--SO WHAT'D YOU HAVE IN MIND?
I'M NOT SURE. BUT I THINK A HAS-BEEN LIKE RISING SUN MIGHT BE EXACTLY THE THING TO SATISFY OUR ESTEEMED BENEFACTORS.
LET'S GET ON THE HORN TO MISTER ITAMI...
...SEE IF WE CAN GET HIM ON BOARD.
IN THE MEANTIME, WE'LL MONITOR HOW THINGS CAN PLAY OUT IN DUBAI...
FINALLY! YOU GUYS DON'T KNOW WHAT YOU'VE BEEN MISSING--!
WELCOME TO THE NEW MECCA OF POP TRASH CULTURE...
@MOSEXSBAT: DUBAI SMELLS LIKE AN OPERATING ROOM. COMPLETELY STERILE.
about 2 minutes ago from Twitteratti

...THE DUBAI ENTERTAINMENT CITY CELEBRATION CENTER! PRETTY SOON EVERY MAJOR CONVENTION WILL CALL THIS MEGA-HALL HOME!
BUT TALK ABOUT A P.R. COUP-- THE SUPER YOUNG TEAM FANFEST EXTRAVAGANZA IS THE FIRST!
WE ARE? AFTER WHAT HAPPENED IN LAS VULGAR--
-- THIS IS ALL JUST DAMAGE CONTROL, ISN'T IT?
Don't forget, Kim...we never got credit for the Oxy-Gen bust. As usual.
WELL, THEY CAN'T COVER THIS UP, CAN THEY?
RIGHT, AHHH...WELL, THAT'S THE IDEA, LANTERN BOY.
I'VE SAID IT FROM DAY ONE-- WE NEED TO SHOW THE ENTIRE WORLD JUST HOW SPECIAL YOU ARE. HOW YOU CROSS ALL CULTURAL LINES...!
I DON'T KNOW, HEINO. I THINK TAKUMI OTOMO'S GOT A BETTER PITCH THAN THIS GUY.
HIS TALENTS ARE INFINITELY INTANGIBLE, NO DOUBT...
...BUT I FIGURE I'M RICH ENOUGH TO TRY ANYTHING ONCE.
superyoungteam
-superyoungte
canary
superbat
shiny happy
@MOSEXSBAT: FINALLY BEING EXPLOITED IN THE MANNER IN WHICH WE'RE ACCUSTOMED.
about 5 seconds ago from Twitteratti

WE HAVE BEEN WAITING. WE HAVE BEEN PATIENT. AND NOW *OUR* TIME HAS COME.
WE HAVE *TALENTS*. WE HAVE *VISION*. EACH AND EVERY ONE OF US...
...AND WE LOOK PERFECT. WIR SIND REIN, BÖSE UND BEREIT ZU BRÜTEN UND UNS ZU VERMEHREN.
OUR SECRET SOCIETY WILL ONCE AGAIN BE CALLED TO ACTION.
WORD IS COMING FROM AMERICA. WE SHALL *BENEFIT* FROM THEIR USUAL INABILITY TO *ACT*.
IT WILL BE A GLORIOUS ACHIEVEMENT--
--ONE WORTHY OF THE P.T.A.!
THE PARASITIC TEUTONS OF ASSIMILATION!
TOMORROW WE PLANT *OUR* FLAG ON THE MOUNTAIN OF INFAMY!

@MOSEXSBAT: THEY WANT US TO HAVE A CERTAIN KIND OF FAME. NOT ALL FAME IS FABULOUS.
about 8 minutes ago from Twitteratti
@MOSEXSBAT: CONCERNED NOW. I CAN'T EVEN ACCESS MY OWN HOME DATABASE. SO IT'S NOT JUST A MEDIA BLACKOUT...
about 6 minutes ago from Twitteratti
MOST EXCELLENT SUPERBAT--
--HOW LONG MUST I HAUNT YOU?! WHEN WILL YOU FINALLY PICK UP THE ULTIMATE HERO MANTLE?!
YOU MUST RISE ABOVE THIS SENSELESS DOLATRY!
HAVE YOU NO PROTECTOR SENSE? HAVE YOU NOT YET REALIZED WHERE YOUR TALENTS ARE NEEDED MOST?!
THE POWER OF ALL THINGS IS WITHIN YOU!

ULTIMON-ALPHA.
DO YOU HAVE INSIGHTS INTO THE CURRENT PLIGHT OF OUR HOMELAND?
YOU WILL RESPECT THE MASTER MONSTER KILLER, BOY! I HAVE INSIGHTS INTO THE ENORMITY OF THE UNIVERSE!
EVEN NOW, THE FORCES OF EVIL ARE PLOTTING AGAINST YOU--!
LOOK, BROTHERS! NOW WE PUT OUR POLITICS INTO PRACTICE! UNSERE MISSION IST UNSER LEBEN.
WE HAVE RECEIVED OUR TARGET INSTRUCTIONS! BEHOLD--
facespace
rumblings
invitations
ACCOUNT INFO [EDIT]
Name: MOST EXCELLENT SUPERBAT
PERSONAL INFO [EDIT]
Looking For: All that there is
ACCOUNT INFO [EDIT]
Name: BIG ATOMIC LANTERN BOY
PERSONAL INFO [EDIT]
Looking For: Love, attention, devotion
ACCOUNT INFO [EDIT]
Name: SHINY HAPPY AQUAZON
PERSONAL INFO [EDIT]
Looking For: Still looking...
ACCOUNT INFO [EDIT]
Name: SHY CRAZY LOLITA CANARY
PERSONAL INFO [EDIT]
Looking For: Absolution
ACCOUNT INFO [EDIT]
Name: WELL-SPOKEN SONIC LIGHTNING FLASH
PERSONAL INFO [EDIT]
Looking For: Continuous forward motion
VMail
InterWeb
--WIR WERDEN DIESE IDIOTISCHEN CLOWNSKINDER ERNIEDRIGEN!
aisle 19
section 220
--AND, APPEARING RIGHT NOW IN AISLE 19, THE NEXT CONTESTANTS OF THE SUPER YOUNG TEAM COSPLAY COMPETITION! COME HAVE YOUR PHOTO TAKEN WITH THE NEXT BEST THING!
HOLD IT! LEMME TAKE A PHOTO FOR MY BLOG--
IS THAT THEM? I CAN'T TELL...
OVER HERE--!
--KIDS LOOK GREAT, DON'T THEY?
--BURGERS ARE SIX BUCKS?!
--WANNA' CHECK OUT THE SUPERBAT BOOTH--
--CHECK OUT THOSE HELMETS--
...NO SHY CRAZY LOLITA CANARY?

--PODCASTING LIVE FROM THE FLOOR OF THE SUPER YOUNG TEAM FANFEST EXTRAVAGANZA AND THE COSTUME TRIBUTES ARE OUT IN FULL FORCE!
NOT TO MENTION THE MERCH YOU CAN PICK UP HERE! FROM BOOTLEGGED EPISODES OF SUPERBAT'S TV SHOW--
--TO OFFICIALLY-SANCTIONED PRODUCTS APPROVED BY THE MEMBERS OF SUPER YOUNG TEAM THEMSELVES!
How come no one's dressed like ME?
OH, I'M SURE THERE'S MORE THAN ONE OF YOUR FANS HANGING AROUND, CANARY.
LET'S FACE IT, WHEN WAS THE LAST TIME THERE WAS A JUSTICE LEAGUE CONVENTION OF THIS SIZE AND SCOPE? THE WHOLE WORLD'S WATCHING...!
EVENT STAFF
EVENT STAFF
WELL, SUPERMAN'S GONE AND BATMAN'S DEAD...
...SOMEONE'S GOT TO STEP UP.
LISTEN, THIS IS THE KIND OF FAN DEVOTION THAT WE NEED EVERYONE TO SEE! I MEAN, NOBODY DRESSES UP AS THE TITANS ANYMORE...!
YOU'RE LIKE THE BEATLES RIGHT BEFORE THEY DID THE SULLIVAN SHOW. THINGS ARE ABOUT TO BUST WIDE OPEN!
THESE KIDS HAVE READ ALL ABOUT YOU! WATCHED YOU ON VIRAL VIDEO! THEY'VE FOLLOWED YOU THROUGH THE UNDERGROUND...
YO. WHO'RE THE BEATLES...?
@MOSEXSBAT: I KNEW I WAS MY OWN FASHION CULT. SOMETIMES YOU FIND ONE FRESH OFF THE RUNWAY.
about 1 second ago from Twitteratti

IT ALL SEEMS GENUINE...
ONLY ONE WAY TO FIND OUT.
WELL-SPOKEN LIGHTNING FLASH. RECONNOITER.
I'MONIT--
--OKAYBACK.
MAINLY VENDORS OF ALL TYPES. EVEN SAW A LEXCORP BOOTH. APPARENTLY, WE'RE BIG BUSINESS.
COOL.
SO THIS PLACE HAS EVERY-THING BUT A REASON FOR US TO BE HERE.

--THIS IS FOR MY BLOG. DO YOU HAVE A FAVORITE SUPER YOUNG TEAM ADVENTURE?
HAVE THEY ACTUALLY HAD ONE? I THOUGHT THEY WERE JUST ANIME CHARACTERS...
...AND I DO IT CAUSE THE BOYS LOVE IT.
?!
--ARE WE GETTING A CUT OF THE BOX OFFICE?!
WELL, WE HAVE A DEAL WITH THE EVENT ORGANIZERS TO--
I'M NOT SURE AN EVENT LIKE THIS MAKES US MORE SPECIAL. IF ANYTHING, IT MAKES US LOOK--
--LESS SPECIAL...
HMMM...
@MOSEXSBAT: I KNOW THE OLD GHOST IS RIGHT, BUT WHEN OPPORTUNITY KNOCKS....
about 1 minute ago from Twitteratti

This is not my kind of shopping spree! And it's not because no one's paying proper tribute to me...!
Where did everybody else go--?!
SO, YOU WANT A PRETZEL BAGEL OR MAYBE...
ACTUALLY, WE SHOULD BOTH PROBABLY LOAD UP ON LIQUID REFRESHMENT...
...KNOW WHAT I MEAN?
OH, YES. YOU'RE... SUPPOSED TO BE AQUAZON. I GET IT.
DO IT. DO IT! DO IT!
BET NO ONE'S IN HERE...
...JUST AN EMPTY OFFICE. PERFECT PLACE TO DO SOME BUSINESS, RIGHT...?
SO LET'S TALK SHINY. LET'S TALK HAPPY.
NOT QUITE SURE WHAT YOUR LINE IS SUPPOSED TO--
--MMMFFF??

DON'T BE NERVOUS...
@MOSEXSBAT: THERE IS NO SMOOTHER LINE THAN MINE.
about 5 minutes ago from Twitteratti
...YOU KNOW WHAT I'M ALL ABOUT. I DON'T HIDE ANYTHING EXCEPT FOR MY SECRET IDENTITY.
YOU TRY AND DRESS LIKE ME? WEAR MY COLORS OUT IN PUBLIC?
LET'S CONSIDER EXACTLY WHAT THAT MEANS. RIGHT NOW. IN THIS MOMENT.
I THINK YOU CAME HERE LOOKING FOR SOMETHING... SOMETHING SACRED...
NOW STAND UP.
GANZA
ECTIBLES
PARDONME.
EXCUSEME-PLEASE.
SORRY.
LEXBOX 720
WAYSTATIC
UT--
HA! THE JUGENDTREFFEN HAS JUSTIFIED ITS EXISTENCE! ONE OF THEM IS REVEALED!
BRÜDER! ASSIMILIEREN UND ZERSTÖREN SIE!

@MOSEXSBAT:
SOMETIMES DREAMS CAN COME TRUE.
about 10 seconds ago from Twitteratti

GET OFF--!

C'MON... YOU DO KNOW YOUR WAY AROUND...
BIG... ATOMIC...

H-HEY, "LIGHTNING FLASH"...PACE YOURSELF...
NFF!
AHHH... LITTLE TO THE LEFT...

I'm just saying it shouldn't be that difficult to replicate my--
?!
Don't tell me someone's trying to upstage--
--oh.

FIRST STEP: COMPLETE! WE HAVE TAKEN HIS UNIQUENESS!
NEXT STEP: PENDING! WE WILL TAKE HIS LIFE!
ICH BIN SCHNELL!
CANARY?
DID YOU HEAR THAT...?!
THAT WASN'T YOU...?
@MOSEXSBAT: FROM A WHISPER TO A SCREAM.
SOME THINGS ARE BETTER LEFT UNSAID.
about 2 seconds ago from Twitteratti

Oh! *Lightning Flash!* I didn't know--
PLEASE--DON'T APOLOGIZE...! MY EARS COULDN'T TAKE IT...
MAYBE YOU SHOULDN'T HAVE *DONE* THAT...
AND *ANOTHER ONE* IS EXPOSED!
DEMONSTRATION OF SKILL MAKES THEM IMMEDIATELY *VULNERABLE!* NOW WE HAVE THE POWER--
ONE BY ONE--SEE HOW THEY *FALL?*
P.T.A.! P.T.A.! P.T.A.!
TRIUMPH DES WIRD!

ACH--?!
SNEAK ATTACK?!
NOT SO SNEAKY.
WHO'RE THESE GUYS SUPPOSED TO BE DRESSED LIKE...?
EVEN YOUR ARROGANCE IS CONTAGIOUS!
HEY--!
THE P.T.A. ARE SCIENTIFIC MIRACLES! ENGINEERED TO FORCIBLY TAKE WHAT IS UNIQUE IN OTHERS!
AND TO RETURN IN KIND--

GAH--!
HEY...I THINK THAT'S ENOUGH--
LISTEN-- N-NO...I'VE GOT TO--
C'MON, BABY--
YOU KNOW YOU WANTED THIS...
I SAID--

--NO MEANS NO!

--STILL PODCASTING LIVE FROM THE FLOOR! IT'S BECOME LIFE OR DEATH DOWN HERE! THE CON HAS BEEN OVERRUN BY... I DUNNO...TENNIS NAZIS!
ON THE PLUS SIDE, WE'RE ACTUALLY SEEING SUPER YOUNG TEAM IN ACTION--

--MAYBE FOR THE VERY FIRST TIME!

WATCH IT, BORIS BECKER!
YOU'VE GOT THE WRONG GIRL--!
YOU WEAR THEIR DISGUISE--YOU SHARE THEIR FATE!

WHOA! OKAY, WE'RE GOING TO PICK THIS UP FROM OUTSIDE THE HALL--!
YEE-OOWWW--!
WHAT'S THE MATTER WITH YOU?! IS THIS AN ADMISSION OF DEFEAT?!
YOU MEN ARE THE SHAME OF THE P.T.A.!
ALL IS NOT LOST! WE SHALL RALLY!
WIR SIND DAS SCHÖNE! WE CANNOT BE DEFEATED BY MERE--
--GUH--!
WOW...NOW THERE'S A FAN COSTUME.
It's about time--!

I WAS STUCK IN MY HOTEL ROOM. HAD SOME TROUBLE GETTING THE WINGS ON STRAIGHT.
DID I MISS ANYTHING GOOD...?
THIS IS A NIGHTMARE--
--WHO DO YOU PEOPLE THINK YOU ARE?! DON'T YOU GET IT?! WE'RE THE SUPERHEROES!
YOU! YOU'RE NOT SHY! YOU'RE NOT CRAZY! YOU'RE NOT EVEN SORRY!
AND YOU! IS THIS YOUR PATHETIC ATTEMPT TO BE SOME SORT OF HOT LOVER MAN?!
WH-WHAT? ARE YOU REFERRING TO--
ENOUGH NONSENSE!
AS FOR YOU--
--I'M SO OVER YOU!
HUH?!
WOW.
THE WHOLE THING IS COMPLETELY WRECKED. LIKE SOMEONE DROPPED A BOMB...
WHAT HAPPENED...?
@MOSEXSBAT:
SOMETIMES I FEEL NOTHING.
about 1 minute ago from Twitteratti
THE GOOD OL' USA:

GLAD YOU COULD MAKE IT, MISTER YASUNARI. THESE HYPERSONIC SIGNALS...YOU NEVER KNOW IF THEY ACTUALLY GET *HEARD*.
BUT YOU'RE HERE AND WE'RE THRILLED. WE KNOW YOU HAVE CONCERNS ABOUT THE STATE OF YOUR HOMELAND. WE COMPLETELY UNDERSTAND.

WE WORK WITH MISTER ITAMI. HE WANTED US TO... *CONSOLIDATE* OUR AGENDAS, IF POSSIBLE.
PART OF OUR JOB IS TO TARGET RESOURCES. TO *MAXIMIZE* THEM. YOU, SIR, ARE A *FANTASTIC* RESOURCE.

YOU'VE GOT THE *HISTORY*. YOU'VE GOT THE ATTITUDE. YOU'VE GOT THE *COSTUME*. TOGETHER, WE CAN...
MISTER YASUNARI...?
UMMM...
IS THERE SOMETHING *WRONG*...?
NOT AT ALL. I APPRECIATE YOUR INTEREST.
BUT I HAVE ALREADY PARTNERED WITH SOMEONE SLIGHTLY MORE AMBITIOUS...

...AND WE HAVE OUR *OWN* PLANS FOR MAXIMIZING MY RESOURCES.

OKAY, THIS IS REALLY WEIRD...
NO ANSWER AT I.C., INC. NOT EVEN A *RECEPTIONIST* PICKING UP...
WHEN IT RAINS, IT POURS...
OKAY, LET'S TALK ABOUT HOW WE CAN *SPIN* THIS. I MEAN, OBVIOUSLY YOU GUYS SAVED THE DAY. WELL, SORT OF...
WE DID NOTHING. AS USUAL. AND I'M BEGINNING TO THINK THIS ARRANGEMENT ISN'T WORKING OUT.
YOU SAID IT, HEINO...
...BUT I REALLY DON'T THINK IT'S GOING TO GET ANY BETTER. FOR *MYSELF*, I SEE ONLY ONE ALTERNATIVE.
I'M OUT.
KIM...
...YOU *CAN'T*--!
WHAT ARE YOU SAYING...?
I'M SAYING I'M *LEAVING* SUPER YOUNG TEAM. I'M SAYING I'M NOT NEEDED HERE, THAT MUCH IS CLEAR TO ME.
SO THERE.
She's *serious?* She's taking a solo flight?
Are you just going to let this *happen...?!*
WAIT A MINUTE...WAIT A MINUTE...
YES! THIS IS *PERFECT!*

THIS IS EXACTLY WHAT THIS STORY IS MISSING! YOU GUYS HAVEN'T HAD YOUR SECOND ACT YET! YOU NEED TO BE LAID LOW! THE GLITZ AND GLAMOUR STRIPPED AWAY!
THE PUBLIC'LL EAT UP THIS KIND OF INTERPERSONAL DRAMA--
--THEY LOVE TO SEE THEIR HEROES TORN DOWN!
BUT... I'M TOTALLY SERIOUS...
YEAH, WELL... SURE. MAKES SENSE TO ME.
I MEAN... WHAT'S THE POINT IN STICKING AROUND ANYWAY?
Oh, come on, Boy. You're an open book...!
WHAT DO YOU SAY, LIGHTNING FLASH...?
WHATEVER.
I GUESS.
FAN-TASTIC! YOU COULDN'T ASK FOR A BETTER SETUP FOR THE BIG COMEBACK! THE SHOT HEARD 'ROUND THE WORLD--
--SUPER YOUNG TEAM HAS BROKEN UP!
NEXT DANCE MOVE:

CHAPTER FOUR

ChrisCross & Eduardo Pansica ▮ Pencillers
Rob Stull, Wayne Faucher & Sando Ribeiro ▮ Inkers

dance

OH, IT WAS BEAUTIFUL. PURE P.R. POETRY. HAD AN ENTIRE ENTERTAINMENT NEWS CYCLE TO OURSELVES. YOU'D THINK THE JUSTICE LEAGUE CALLED IT QUITS AGAIN...!
NO...AS FAR AS I KNOW, THEY'RE SCATTERED TO THE FOUR WINDS...
SYT SYT SYT
SYT SYT SYT
TRUST ME, THEY'LL LAY LOW... AS INSTRUCTED. THEY KNOW THE POWER OF A PUBLIC COMEBACK.
WHO, ME? I'M HEADED UP TO INNOVATIVE CONCEPTS. I'VE BEEN FORCED TO GROK A FACE-TO-FACE...
I KNOW! CAN YOU BELIEVE IT?! BUT WHAT CHOICE DO I HAVE?
THEY GAVE ME THE AUTONOMY TO BREAK THIS TEAM UP...BUT THEY'VE BEEN RADIO SILENT FOR DAYS...!
SYT SYT SYT
SYT SYT SYT
...
OKAY, THAT'S WEIRD.
NO RECEPTIONIST, EVEN.
MAYBE I UNDERESTIMATED HOW BAD THE ECONOMY'S BEEN...
...EVEN THESE FAT CATS HAVE BEEN--
...
--LEMME CALL YOU BACK...
INTERESTING. YOU MAY NOT BE ONE OF THEM...

behind the muzak
...BUT YOU'VE GOT THEIR STINK ON YOU.
PLEASE... JOIN US.

@MOSEXSBAT: I ALWAYS WANTED MY OWN PRIVATE ISLAND OFF THE COAST OF JAPAN.
about 8 minutes ago from Twitteratti
@MOSEXSBAT: SO I PAID TO HAVE ONE BUILT.
about 7 minutes ago from Twitteratti
@MOSEXSBAT: ON IT, I CONSTRUCTED THE MOST SERENE SANCTUARY.
about 5 minutes ago from Twitteratti
@MOSEXSBAT: AND UNDERNEATH, MY MOST EXCELLENT SUPERBAT-CAVE.
about 4 minutes ago from Twitteratti
@MOSEXSBAT: I PULLED A SOUVENIR FROM THE "BRAIN DRAIN" ESCAPADE...
about 3 minutes ago from Twitteratti
@MOSEXSBAT: ...WE WERE MICROSCOPIC SUPERPEOPLE. I HELD THE ORIGINAL CONTROL CELL IN MY TINY HANDS...
about 3 minutes ago from Twitteratti
@MOSEXSBAT: ...YOU NEVER KNOW WHEN YOU'LL NEED TO COP A RAY PALMER AGAIN.
about 3 minutes ago from Twitteratti
@MOSEXSBAT: WHEN THE OPPORTUNITY ARISES, I WON'T REPEAT THE SAME MISTAKES. I'LL MAKE ALL NEW ONES.
about 1 minute ago from Twitteratti
THIS IS HOW YOU HONOR A GREAT TRADITION--
--BY LETTING IT ALL *FALL APART?!*
ADVERSITY BREEDS TRIUMPH! EMBRACE YOUR TRANS-GRESSIONS!
ULTIMON-ALPHA. WE MUST STOP MEETING LIKE THIS.
IS EVERY OLD GHOST A SUPER-LIFE COACH?
ARE YOU INDEED THE HERO OF YOUR OWN DREAMS?
THEN *ACT* LIKE IT.

WELCOME TO FUJI STATION, SHINY HAPPY AQUAZON. WE GREET YOU WITH OPEN ARMS AND WARM HEARTS.
HERE SHE IS.
ONLY FOUR HOURS LATE.
APOLOGIES, FATHER. I... MISPLACED THE FREQUENCY GENERATOR.
COULDN'T GET A SIGNAL LOCK ON YOUR TRANSPORT SYSTEM--
NO NEED FOR *EXCUSES*...
...YOU WILL SOON LEARN THAT THINGS RUN *DIFFERENTLY* HERE THAN WITH YOUR YOUNG FRIENDS.
YOU UNDERSTAND?
YES.
THEN LET ME MAKE PROPER *INTRODUCTIONS*, ALTHOUGH YOU SHOULD ALREADY BE *FAMILIAR* WITH THEM--
--YOUR NEW COMPANIONS IN JAPAN'S MOST HONORABLE HERO TEAM, *BIG SCIENCE ACTION*:
HAMMERSUIT ZERO-X. ONE OF THE ORIGINALS. A TECHNOLOGICAL MARVEL THAT IS WALKING PROOF OF JAPAN'S TECHNICAL SUPERIORITY.
MOST KIND, SENIOR WAVEMAN.
BOSS BISHONEN IS THE SUCCESSOR TO THE VENERABLE BOSS BOSOZUKO. HE CARRIES THE TORCH OF A GRAND TRADITION OF FIERY CHAMPIONS.
SO TO SPEAK.
AND *NAZO BALUDA* IS OUR DARK STAR STEALTH WARRIOR. SHE WAS OUR *NEWEST* RECRUIT...

...UNTIL NOW, OF COURSE.
M-MOST HONORED.
JAPAN HAS NEVER NEEDED US MORE THAN RIGHT NOW.
EVEN OUR ORIGINAL SQUAD NEVER FACED SUCH CHALLENGES.
REAL CHALLENGES. NOT P.R. CHALLENGES.
RIGHT.
SO, HAMMERSUIT ZERO...WHAT HAPPENED TO MISS KUSANAGI? IS SHE--
STILL IN THE PILOT'S WOMB, DEAR GIRL...
...I'VE HAD THIS SUIT MODIFIED MORE TIMES THAN I CAN COUNT.
I LIKE TO STAY COMPETITIVE.
YOU MAY WANT TO RETHINK YOUR UNIFORM, AQUAZON. THIS ISN'T ABOUT A PHOTO OP.
WHAT KIND OF REMARK IS--
SINCEREST APOLOGIES, CHAMPIONS--
--BIG SCIENCE EMERGENCY!
THEY'RE RIGHT BEHIND ME--!

WHOA--!
RIGHT THERE, BIG SCIENCE!
THE MID NIGHT MONSTER CLUB IS MAKING THEIR FINAL ASSAULT--
--THEY MEAN TO BRING THE BATTLE TO OUR HOME!
RETURN VIOLENCE!
YOU HEARD THE BOSS--
--FIRE UP!

THEY ARE OF ONE MIND.
BACTERIA ON TWO WHEELS.
COSMO RACER IS CORRECT! THE CLUB IS A SINGLE ORGANISM!
SHOW NO MERCY--!
THIS IS SERIOUS...!
HONORED DAUGHTER--
--THERE IS SOMETHING I MUST REVEAL TO YOU! I KNOW YOU HAVE QUESTIONS CONCERNING YOUR ORIGINS!
FOR YOUR OWN GOOD, YOU WERE NEVER TOLD--BUT YOU ARE THE RESUL OF A FORBIDDEN UNION! THAT OF MYSELF--
--AND THE GENIUS DAUGHTER OF MY MENTOR, SENIOR WAVEMAN OTOMO!

I-I THINK... THIS ACTIVATES THE S-SYSTEM...
...THIS IS THE I.C. MEDIA ROOM.
Y-YOU...CAN PRETTY MUCH WATCH THE WHOLE WORLD...FROM IN HERE...
THIS IS EXACTLY WHAT WE NEED TO MOVE FORWARD.
QUICK DECISIONS MUST BE MADE IF WE'RE TO FULLY RETURN AND BEGIN AGAIN.
BEING SCRAPED OFF A BOOT HEEL AND INCUBATED IN FILTERED CACTUS SAP TENDS TO AFFECT ONE'S GENERAL OUTLOOK.
CERTAINLY THINGS HAVE CHANGED SINCE I WAS LAST SO SELF-AWARE.
AHHH...THE ENTIRE PLANET AT OUR FINGERTIPS...

...BUT I SEE THE WORLD HAS BEEN SCARRED. IN SOME WAYS, BEYOND RECOGNITION. THAT COULD BE USED TO OUR ADVANTAGE.
FIND ME THE DEEPEST WOUND WITHIN THESE GEOPOLITICAL BORDERS.
UMMM...I THINK THIS MAP IS INTERACTIVE...
LOOKS LIKE MIDWAY CITY GOT HIT PRETTY HARD...
INDEED.
IT SEEMS THE MANIPULATION OF THIS HOST WAS PREORDAINED... A TOOL TO BE USED TO FURTHER SOME SORT OF SORDID CAPITALISTIC GOAL.
PERHAPS THIS IS WHERE WE MAKE OUR STAND...
...LET THE WORLD KNOW THAT ITS LONG JOURNEY INTO NIGHT HAS JUST BEGUN.
YOU.
YOU MANIPULATE THE PERCEPTION OF EVENTS, DON'T YOU? A WORTHLESS TALENT THAT IS WITHIN YOUR SKILL SET?
GLK!
THEN YOU WILL PRESENT MY INTENTIONS TO THE WORLD.

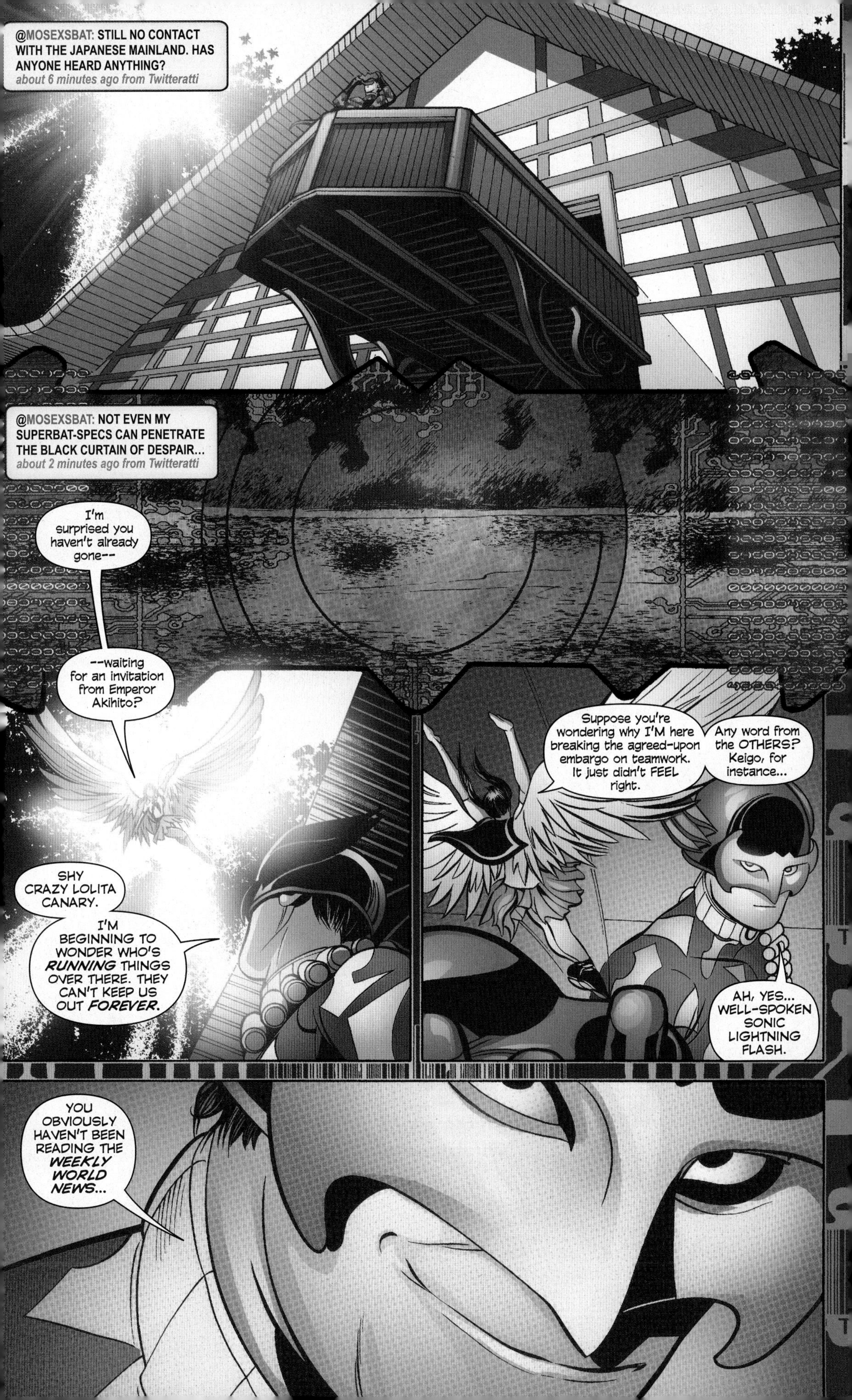
@MOSEXSBAT: STILL NO CONTACT WITH THE JAPANESE MAINLAND. HAS ANYONE HEARD ANYTHING?
about 6 minutes ago from Twitteratti
@MOSEXSBAT: NOT EVEN MY SUPERBAT-SPECS CAN PENETRATE THE BLACK CURTAIN OF DESPAIR...
about 2 minutes ago from Twitteratti
I'm surprised you haven't already gone--
--waiting for an invitation from Emperor Akihito?
SHY CRAZY LOLITA CANARY.
I'M BEGINNING TO WONDER WHO'S RUNNING THINGS OVER THERE. THEY CAN'T KEEP US OUT FOREVER.
Suppose you're wondering why I'M here breaking the agreed-upon embargo on teamwork. It just didn't FEEL right.
Any word from the OTHERS? Keigo, for instance...
AH, YES... WELL-SPOKEN SONIC LIGHTNING FLASH.
YOU OBVIOUSLY HAVEN'T BEEN READING THE WEEKLY WORLD NEWS...

"...KEIGO DISCOVERED THE DESERTS OF AMERICA AND DECIDED HE WOULD SIMPLY TAKE A WALK.
"AND HE NEVER STOPPED.
"EVEN NOW, HE HAS GATHERED FOLLOWERS WHO KEEP IN PERFECT STEP JUST TEN FEET BEHIND HIM. WHERE HE GOES, THEY GO."
"To what END, though?"
"WHO CAN REALLY EXPLAIN THE LURE OF A FAD? IF THEY BELIEVE THIS ENDLESS WALK LEADS TO SOME SORT OF ENLIGHTENMENT, THEN SO BE IT."
...STILL BUZZING ABOUT THE SUDDEN BREAK-UP OF SUPER YOUNG TEAM. SO MUCH UNFULFILLED PROMISE FROM THESE JAPANESE HERO IMPORTS, AND NOT A WORD SINCE...
WE WERE SOLD THIS BILL OF GOODS BASED ON OUR PERCEIVED NATIONAL LOYALTIES. AND YET, WHY WOULD THEY KEEP US IN THE DARK ABOUT OUR COUNTRY'S STATUS AND ENGINEER A WORLDWIDE PHENOMENON IN OUR NAME?
THE REACTION TO OUR DISSOLUTION HAS ME CURIOUS.
I hear it's a DRY heat there.

EVERY CORPORATE STRATEGY IS MERELY A DAISY CHAIN OF DECISIONS AND FACELESS BUREAUCRACY. BUT TO ACTUALLY PUT A *FACE* TO IT...
I BELIEVE IN THE THETA STATE. I BELIEVE IN PRANIC DISCOVERY.
THE MOST SERENE SANCTUARY CONTAINS A UNIFIED DATA FIELD. I ACCESS IT THROUGH OPTIMUM MEDITATIVE TECHNIQUES.
I'M SEARCHING JUSTIN HANOVER'S LIFE. EVERY ELECTRONIC BIT OF INFORMATION THAT *EXISTS* WHERE HE IS CONCERNED...
What are you trying to learn?
You...don't have a WET BAR down here, do you...?
...AND *HERE* IS THE ANSWER, SCROLLING AT THE SPEED OF THOUGHT: HIS *EMPLOYER*.
A COMPANY CALLED *INNOVATIVE CONCEPTS*. BRANCH OFFICES ALL OVER THE WORLD...INCLUDING *TOKYO*.
NOW YOU'RE FULFILLING YOUR POTENTIAL!
TREAD WHERE ANGELS FEAR! PLACE YOUR FOOTPRINTS ON THE ROCK OF MONSTER ISLE!
@MOSEXSBAT: TO BE GHOSTLY IS TO BE OBTUSE. IF I EVER DIE, I WILL MAINTAIN STRICT RADIO SILENCE.
about 10 seconds ago from Twitteratti
SYT SYT
SYT SYT

@MOSEXSBAT: TO ADVERTISE ONESELF IS TO ADVERTISE ONE'S OWN NAÏVETÉ.
about 3 seconds ago from Twitteratti
SYT SYT SYT
BUT...I DIDN'T GET TO DO ANYTHING...
ANYONE THINK THIS WAS JUST THE FIRST WAVE? ARE THERE MORE COMING...?
ONBOARD DATA STREAM SHOWING RECRUITMENT FOR THE CLUB IS WAY DOWN. THANKFULLY, THIS COULD BE IT.
THEN WE HAVE BEATEN DOWN THE ABERRATIONS OF HUMANITY. A RIGHTEOUS VICTORY FOR BIG SCIENCE ACTION.
FEAR NOT, DAUGHTER. SOON ENOUGH YOU WILL STAND BESIDE US TO FACE THE EVIL BEASTS OF THIS WORLD. FOR NOW...
...LET US ADJOURN TO THE BIG SCIENCE CONFERENCE CENTER FOR IMMEDIATE DEBRIEFING.
ASSESSMENTS MUST BE MADE IN PREPARATION FOR ADDITIONAL THREATS THAT MIGHT HAVE SHAKEN LOOSE IN THE RECENT UPHEAVAL.
WHAT HAS HAPPENED HERE, FATHER?
WE WERE UNABLE TO ACCESS ANY INFORMATION CONCERNING THE HEALTH AND WELFARE OF OUR HOMELAND...
WE ARE OFFLINE.
SO BE IT.

CLEARLY THE STATE OF OUR NATION DEMANDS OUR STRICT COMPLIANCE WITH OUR LEADERS' WISHES. FOR NOW, WE ARE COVERT.
HAVE THEY GIVEN US ANY REASON NOT TO ALERT THE WORLD THAT JAPAN IS UNDER OUR PROTECTION...?
THEY HAVE NOT. CURIOUS, BUT WE DO NOT QUESTION THE EMPEROR OR ANY OF OUR GOVERNMENT OFFICIALS.
WE ARE SILENT CHAMPIONS GUARDING THE GATES...
...AND, AS YOU ALL KNOW, WE SEEK NEITHER RECOGNITION NOR GLORY.
SUBTLE DIG.
COSMO RACER. WHAT OF THE NORTH KOREANS...?
THE WORKERS' PARTY BATTALION HAS NOT MOBILIZED AS OF YET. LIKEWISE, THE JUCHE KING AND THE ETERNAL COMMANDER REMAIN DORMANT IN THEIR SILOS.
YET THEY MUST SUSPECT OUR WEAKNESS...
...PERHAPS OUR LEADERS' TACTICS OF SOCIAL DIVERSION ARE ACTUALLY WORKING.

@MOSEXSBAT:
I BRANDED MYSELF SUPERHERO. NOW I AM BRANDED VIGILANTE. GRIM AND GRITTY.
about 2 minutes ago from Twitteratti
MADNESS!
Our own military is FIRING on us! WHY?!
OBVIOUSLY, THEY REALLY DON'T WANT US TO SEE WHAT'S OCCURRED THERE. WHICH ONLY MAKES ME WANT TO SEE IT MORE...
...BUT THAT REVELATION CAN WAIT FOR ANOTHER DAY.
I HAVE NO INTEREST IN HUMILIATING OUR COUNTRYMEN.
FOR NOW, MY SUPERHERO SLEUTHING ABILITIES DEMAND TO BE PUT TO THE TEST.
SETTING COURSE FOR THE LAND OF THE FREE.

@MOSEXSBAT: CORPORATE. MONOLITHIC. NONDESCRIPT. INNOVATIVE CONCEPTS.
about 12 minutes ago from Twitteratti
I just realized something, Heino...
...we're participating in illegal activity.
REFER TO ME ONLY AS MOST EXCELLENT SUPERBAT IN THE FIELD.
I HAVE SEDUCED THIS BUILDING AS I WOULD A TEENAGED FANGIRL.
IT HAS REVEALED ALL ITS INNERMOST SECRETS UNTO ME.
SECURITY PASS CODE: MAXWELL THE FOURTH--
ACKNOWLEDGED AND ACCEPTED. ALL BUILDING SECURITY SYSTEMS: DEACTIVATED.
Now what?
NOW WE TRACE THE EMERGENT DATA STREAMS TO A CENTRAL C.P.U., THE SOURCE OF ALL CORPORATE INTEL WHERE THIS COMPANY IS CONCERNED...
...AND THERE IT IS. RIGHT HERE INSIDE THE BUILDING.
PREPARE FOR IMMERSIVE TECH-DIVING.

@MOSEXSBAT: SOMEWHAT OLD-FASHIONED. SOON IT'LL ALL BE FLUID MOLECULE CHAIN STORAGE.
about 2 seconds ago from Twitteratti
WE NEED COMPLETE ACCESS.
THAT MEANS PENETRATING THIS MACHINE-BRAIN THROUGH INTERRUPTIVE SURGERY.
REPLACE THE ALPHA CHIP WITH THE SUPERBAT SPECIAL...
...AND WE WILL FORGE A NEW RELATIONSHIP: MASTER AND SLAVE.
We find romance anywhere we can.
These execs enjoy their liquid lunches, don't they...?
@MOSEXSBAT: THEY CALL THIS A TV ROOM? SMALL MINDS DESIGNED THIS PIT.
about 1 minute ago from Twitteratti
Welcome to Pandora's Box.
Shall we?
INDEED WE SHALL.
BEGIN INFO-SURF: NOW.

--RANDOM FLAME PATTERNS SEEN OVER THE PACIFIC. METEOROLOGISTS AREN'T RULING OUT METAHUMAN ACTIVITY.
THIS WAS OF SOME INTEREST TO THEM...
Who do we know who ACTS OUT like that...?
RISING SUN.
POOR OLD MAN.
HERE'S SOME MORE OLD VID FROM THEIR COMMUNICATIONS ARCHIVE...
Wait. Who is THAT...?
I RECOGNIZE HIM. FROM THE SATELLITE...
WE HIRED YOU TO USE THESE FALSE IDOLS TO DISTRACT THE WORLD FROM THE CURRENT PLIGHT OF OUR HOME-LAND!
THEY HAVE THEIR OWN BRAND OF AMBITION...WHICH MAKES THEM VERY DANGEROUS--
--THE WORLD MUST NEVER KNOW THE TRUTH ABOUT JAPAN. EVEN OUR OWN CITIZENS MUST NOT KNOW.

THESE RIDICULOUS COSTUMES AND THEIR OUTLANDISH MONIKERS... HOPEFUL OF ACCEPTANCE IN THE WEST...THEY ARE COMMODITIES. AND WE WILL TREAT THEM AS SUCH.
RISING SUN IS THE PERFECT FOIL. A GENERATIONAL CONFLICT WILL AMUSE THE WORLD AND STIR UP DEBATE THAT HAS NOTHING TO DO WITH THE HORRORS THAT OUR NATION IS ACTUALLY DEALING WITH.
PRIZE FIGHTS OCCUR WHERE THEY ARE NEEDED MOST. THIS WILL BE A CHAMPIONSHIP BOUT ON THE WORLD STAGE.
BY THE TIME THESE TWO PLAY OUT THEIR EGOCENTRIC KABUKI PERFORMANCE...
...OUR RECOVERY WILL BE COMPLETE.
OUR HONOR RESTORED.
RIGHT.
THEY HAVE THEIR PLANS. WE HAVE OURS.
SUPER YOUNG TEAM MUST REUNITE IMMEDIATELY.
So...Keigo's in the desert. Kim is with her father.
What about Big Atomic Lantern Boy?
THAT IS A MOST EXCELLENT QUESTION.

I KNOW HOW YOU FEEL, KID...
...I HAD TO LIVE UP TO BOSOZUKO'S LEGEND, TOO. IT WASN'T EASY.
MY RECRUITMENT WAS EMOTIONAL, AS WELL. LUCKILY, I WAS NEEDED FOR THE SIEGE ON THE SCARRBA CLAN.
SOME GIRLS HAVE ALL THE LUCK.
WHO KNOWS? ONE DAY YOU MAY BE RUNNING THINGS.
AS LONG AS YOU DON'T RELOCATE B.S.A. TO AN ABANDONED MITSUBISHI MOTOR PLANT. THAT NEVER WORKS.
SO VERY FUNNY.
TELL ME, BOSS...ARE YOU A MALE OR A FEMALE?
I'M ASSUMING IF YOU TRULY VALUED YOUR CELEBRITY STATUS, YOU WOULDN'T BE HERE.
I HAD TO DROP MY OWN FETISH INTERESTS WHEN I JOINED UP.
MUCH TO OUR CHAGRIN, NAZO...
...BUT HEROES OF OUR VENERABLE NATURE MUST CULTIVATE OTHER, LOFTIER INTERESTS.
THERE IS NO TIME FOR FRIVOLOUS DRAMA...

DID...I MAKE IT...?
IS THIS...FUJI STATION? HOME OF BIG SCIENCE ACTION?
NOT BAD.
PERHAPS I WILL BE ABLE TO FIND KIM WITHOUT ACTUALLY HAVING TO--
--?!
SO THIS IS WHAT IT'S COME TO...
...YOU'VE BECOME ANOTHER CREEPY STALKER.
BIG MISTAKE, BOY.
NEXT DANCE MOVE:

CHAPTER FIVE

Eduardo Pansica ▮ Penciller
Sandro Ribeiro ▮ Inker

THIS IS SUPPOSED TO BE THE FUTURE OF OUR RIGHTEOUS HEROIC TRADITION...?

UHHHNNN...
KAFF! KOFF!
P-TUH--!
ACK! WHU--
YOU SHOW GREAT DISRESPECT BY COMING HERE UNINVITED...

...BIG SCIENCE TEAM ACCESS ONLY. BUT THAT SHOULD BE OBVIOUS.
SENIOR WAVEMAN SETS POLICY, BOY.
SO YOU WEAR THE SYMBOL OF THE COSMIC LANTERN, BUT YOU ARE NOT ONE OF THEM...

SUCH A M-MASTER OF THE OBVIOUS... COSMO RACER SAN.
STILL ON THE LOOKOUT FOR YOUR "BELOVED MAKER"...?

YOU'VE GOT A MOUTH ON YOU. YOU'RE PLAYING WITH FIRE, KID. COULD LEAD TO A NASTY BURN--
MEET THE NEW BOSS...SAME AS THE OLD BOSS, EH, BISHONEN?
USUALLY, THE EX-MEMBERS OF SUPER YOUNG TEAM PRIDE THEMSELVES ON IMPROVISING ON THE SIDE OF COOL...

...HOWEVER, BIG ATOMIC LANTERN BOY OFTEN PROVES HIMSELF THE EXCEPTION.
HARSH.
I ONLY CAME HERE TO MAKE SURE YOU WERE ALL RIGHT, AQUAZON...

...YOU ONCE SAID FOLLOWING IN YOUR FATHER'S FOOTSTEPS IN B.S.A. WOULD BE A LAST RESORT.
YOU... REMEMBERED THAT...?

THIS IS INTOLERABLE. WE ARE JAPAN'S FIRST LINE OF DEFENSE! WE *EMBODY* THE HERO TRADITION!
AND WITHOUT THE BENEFIT OF PRESS AGENTS--
FATHER...
...I'D RATHER NOT EMBARRASS HIM FURTHER. HE OBVIOUSLY HAS NOWHERE ELSE TO GO.
IF AT ALL POSSIBLE, CAN WE JUST--
HONORED DAUGHTER. YOU MUST *EMBRACE* THE FACT THAT, OF *ALL* YOUR YOUNG COMPANIONS, *YOU* ARE THE LEGACY MEMBER.
YOUR FATE AMONG BIG SCIENCE ACTION WAS SEALED THE MOMENT YOU WERE BORN. THESE *OTHER* IMPUDENT CHILDREN...
...THEY ARE NOT *WELCOME*. NOR ARE THEY--
OH NO...
...STRANGE BEHAVIOR ON DECK.
THIS...THIS IS *NOT* MY DOING--
HE IS PREPARING TO *ATTACK*--!
I KNEW IT! HE ONLY *FEIGNS* INCOMPETENCE--
GYAAHHH--!

MAXIMUM SHOWMANSHIP...
FORGIVE THE INTRUSION, HONORED ELDERS...
...BUT MOST EXCELLENT SUPERBAT REQUIRES AN IMMEDIATE AUDIENCE WITH HIS EX-TEAMMATES.
HENCE I HAVE APPROPRIATED A LOW ENERGY COMMUNICATION FREQUENCY LOCATED WITHIN THE AVAILABLE SPECTRUM OF ATOMIC LANTERN BOY'S CHEST BEAMER.
WE ARE AN ORGANIZATION IN CRISIS.
@MOSEXSBAT: THERE'S AN INTIMACY TO BE FOUND IN A FACE-TO-HOLOGRAPHIC-FACE MEETING.
about 2 minutes ago from Twitteratti
RECENT INVESTIGATIONS HAVE UNCOVERED A DASTARDLY PLOT TO MANIPULATE US.
THE VERY FORCES WHO CLAIMED TO SHEPHERD US AVE THEIR OWN AGENDA. WE HAVE BEEN USED AND ABUSED.
NOW THE TIME HAS COME TO PROVE ONCE AND FOR
...A GRAND ASCENSION TO GLORY IN THE FACE OF--
SAVE IT, HEINO.
THESE GUYS INVENTED THE LONG-WINDED HERO-SPEECH. THEY'VE HEARD IT ALL.

AND, WORSE, THESE ATROCITIES HAVE OCCURRED IN YOUR OWN BACKYARD, BIG SCIENCE!
PERHAPS THE ABSENCE OF GIANT, REPTILIAN PREDATORS AND SUBTERRANEAN INVADERS PRECLUDE YOU FROM SEEING THEM.
INSOLENT POSER! SHOW SOME RESPECT!

RISING SUN WAS RIGHT ABOUT YOU! WHEN YOU HAVE SAVED JAPAN FROM EXTINCTION ON COUNTLESS OCCASIONS...ONLY THEN CAN YOU CLAIM BRAGGING RIGHTS...!
I-I THOUGHT...IT WASN'T ABOUT EGO, HAMMERSUIT ZERO-X...
BUT IT IS, LANTERN BOY. THE SUPER-EGO OF THE FUTURE.
I'VE GOT PLANS. I'VE GOT SCHEMES.
SURE YOU DO...
...BUT I WANT SOMETHING IN RETURN THIS TIME. LET'S TALK CONCESSIONS.
DAUGHTER! WHAT ARE YOU CONTEMPLATING?!
I NEED YOU HERE...AT MY SIDE...
ALL YOU NEED IS LOVE, FATHER.
WHAT MADNESS IS THIS?! I THOUGHT YOU--
YOU NEVER TRULY ASKED. I HAVE MY OWN SOUL TO EXPLOIT.
BESIDES, YOU'VE NEVER SOLD OUT BUDOKAN SIX NIGHTS IN A ROW...

THERE'S YOUR WAY, FATHER...AND THERE'S OUR WAY. I DOUBT THAT EITHER ONE IS THE CORRECT WAY.
THE WORLD DOESN'T NEED SUPER-HEROES. WE'RE THE ONES WHO NEED A WORLD TO PROTECT...
...OTHERWISE, WE'RE JUST AN OUTMODED CONCEPT THAT'S WAY PAST ITS SELL DATE.
PROFOUND.
WATCHING YOUTH STRUGGLE WITH IDENTITY IS QUITE...
...UNCOMFORTABLE.
WRAP IT IN WHATEVER EMOTIONS YOU CHOOSE, AQUAZON. IF YOU WANT TO MAKE A SCENE, GO RIGHT AHEAD. I'VE ALREADY MADE PLANS TO ADDRESS OUR SUB-PLOTS AND SOAP OPERA...
YOU ARE THE FIRST. IF YOU RETURN, THE OTHERS WILL, TOO.
YOU'RE PATHOLOGICAL, HEINO. BUT I'LL TAKE WHAT I CAN GET.
APOLOGIES, FATHER. I KNOW YOU HAD HIGH HOPES, BUT I AM FOREVER A NON-TRADITIONALIST...
...AND I SUPPOSE IF I'M GOING TO FIND MY OWN WAY, I NEED COMPANIONS WHO I CAN RELATE TO.
EVEN IF I HAVE GROWN TO ACTIVELY DISLIKE THEM.
M-MUCH THANKS, KIM.
I THINK.
EXCELLENT.
BUT THE RECONCILIATION OF SUPER YOUNG TEAM HAS ONLY JUST BEGUN.
WAG THE DUCK

MIDWAY CITY:
YOU HEARD ABOUT WHAT THEY *DID*...
...THEY BLEW OFF MY *UNION* REP WHEN THEY NEGOTIATED THIS DEAL! I MEAN...THIS STUFF COULD BE RADIOACTIVE OR *WORSE*--!
FORGET THE UNION REPS! IF THE *JUSTICE LEAGUE* IS SPONSORING THE CLEANUP EFFORTS, WE'RE COVERED.
JUST DON'T THINK TOO HARD ABOUT WHO'S *IN* THE JUSTICE LEAGUE THESE DAYS. ALL *THAT'LL* DO IS MAKE YOU--
JEEZ--!
WHAT THE *HELL*--?!
INTERESTING TO SEE IT UP CLOSE.
SO MANY *SCARS* THAT STILL REMAIN...
...SO MANY OLD WOUNDS STILL *WIDE OPEN*.

SOMETIMES YOU NEED A LITTLE HELP. SOMEONE TO TALK TO. EVEN SUPERHEROES.
AS A LICENSED THERAPIST, I'VE TREATED BOTH SUPERMAN AND THE MARTIAN MANHUNTER. TRUE, ONE HAS LEFT EARTH AND THE OTHER IS DEAD--
--BUT I'LL STILL TREAT ANY SUPERHERO OPEN TO THE PROCESS OF IN-DEPTH ANALYSIS...
...TODAY, ON--
Dr. Claíre
WE'RE HERE WITH JAPAN'S SUPER YOUNG TEAM. FIVE COLORFUL KIDS MAKING THEIR BID FOR SUPERHERO IMMORTALITY.
BUT, APPARENTLY, THERE'S SOME DYSFUNCTION WITHIN THIS GROUP OF MEDIA SENSATIONS.
TODAY ON THE SHOW, WE'RE GOING TO CRACK THEM OPEN AND SEE WHAT'S INSIDE...
@MOSEXSBAT: DESPERATE MEASURES. IF IT'S NOT ON CAMERA, IT'S NOT REAL.
about 2 hours ago from Twitteratti
SO LET'S TALK. LET'S GET REAL.
YOU WERE LAST SEEN TROLLING THE BYWAYS OF AMERICA...IN SEARCH OF WHAT? PEACE OF MIND? IDENTITY? MEANING?
IT'S NOT LIKE THAT.
IT JUST SEEMED LIKE THE RIGHT THING TO DO. IT WAS ALL INSTINCT.
@MOSEXSBAT: WELL-SPOKEN SONIC LIGHTNING FLASH. WE NEED TO GET HIM RUNNING AGAIN.
about 56 minutes ago from Twitteratti

WE ARE SUPERHEROES. EVERYTHING ELSE IS THE FLOTSAM OF OUR LIFESTYLE.
YOUR HEROES ARE DEAD OR MISSING OR WORSE. SOMEONE HAS TO STEP UP. WHATEVER OUR DIFFERENCES ARE...
...SUPERHEROES MUST RISE ABOVE.
LET'S SEE WHAT THE AUDIENCE THINKS...
UMMM...I'VE NEVER REALLY HEARD OF YOU GUYS...
...BUT IS THERE A WEBSITE WHERE I COULD BUY STUFF? I WANT MY OWN LITTLE WINGED GIRL DOLL...
Hey, I'm not just merchandise...!
Besides, there's a whole new line of reunion-era action figures hitting this Christmas...
@MOSEXSBAT: SHY CRAZY LOLITA CANARY. TINY ALCOHOL BREATH.
about 34 minutes ago from Twitteratti
ACTION FIGURES. I SEE.
SO, IS THIS THE MESSAGE YOU KIDS WANT TO SEND? I'M NOT SURE THE JUSTICE LEAGUE OR THE JUSTICE SOCIETY CONCERN THEMSELVES WITH TIE-IN PRODUCTS...
YOU'VE OBVIOUSLY NEVER BEEN TO KIDDIE LAND IN TOKYO.
THE JLA B@ERBRICKS ARE HUGE. ESPECIALLY THE VIXEN ONE. SO OBVIOUSLY YOU CAN DO BOTH.
NEXT QUESTION.
@MOSEXSBAT: SHINY HAPPY AQUAZON. SHE'S FOUND SOME PERSONAL POWER.
about 22 minutes ago from Twitteratti

OKAY, THEN...LET'S GET DOWN TO IT. WHAT ARE YOU AFTER? TO REUNITE...FINE. YOU'VE DONE THAT.
SO NOW WHAT?
SHE'S PLAYING TO THE CAMERAS.
WE SHOULD'VE DONE OPRAH INSTEAD.
@MOSEXSBAT: BIG ATOMIC LANTERN BOY. LOYALTY OVER LOVE. MOST DAYS, ANYWAY.
about 15 minutes ago from Twitteratti
SUPERHEROES CAN'T JUST SPEND THEIR TIME DOING TV INTERVIEWS AND LICENSING THEIR LIKENESS. OCCASIONALLY, THEY'VE GOT TO STEP UP AND SAVE THE WORLD.
AND, IN MY PROFESSIONAL OPINION, I'M NOT CONVINCED THAT YOU'RE READY TO--
WHAT FRIVOLITY IS THIS?!
THE PLANET IS BURNING AND YOU SUBJECT YOURSELVES TO THIS NIGHTMARE SCENARIO?!
@MOSEXSBAT: THE GHOST OF ULTIMON-ALPHA. FINALLY THEY SEE WHAT'S BEEN HAUNTING ME.
about 10 seconds ago from Twitteratti
SUPER! YOUNG! DESTINY!
Look...it's... it's--
THE GREAT ANCIENT HERO. GLOWING... FLOATING...

YOUR FRAGILITY IS NOT FOR PUBLIC CONSUMPTION! PROJECT NOTHING LESS THAN TOTAL CONFIDENCE AND THE WORLD WILL AGREE!
YOUR DARK NIGHT OF THE SOUL HAS ENDED! THERE ARE MONSTERS TO BE SLAIN!
THIS SAD, PATHETIC DISPLAY... A MOCKERY OF ALL THAT IS--
YOU NEED TO SIGN A RELEASE IF YOU THINK YOU'RE GETTING AIR TIME ON MY SHOW, MISTER--!
ULTIMON! SUPER YOUNG TEAM WILL DO WHAT MUST BE DONE!
WE ARE READY!
THEN BEGONE THESE INSTRUMENTS OF VANITY! THEY ARE THE ANTI-LIGHT OF ILLUMINATION!
FROM BEYOND THE HERE AND NOW...I SUMMON FORTH THE NECESSARY EVENT--!

@MOSEXSBAT: THE O.G. MONSTER KILLER IN ACTION. I AM BOTH STARSTRUCK AND INSPIRED.
about 4 seconds ago from Twitteratti
US, DOESN'T IT?
MOST EXCELLENT SUPERBAT. IF YOU SEEK LEGEND STATUS, BE MINDFUL. THE ENTIRE WORLD NEEDS YOU.
THE HERO'S JOURNEY IS LONG AND ARDUOUS...
...AND ONE NEEDS ALLIES WHO ARE ALSO ON SUCH A PATH.
OF ONE MIND. OF ONE PURPOSE.
NOTHING MORE CAN I TEACH YOU. I HAVE BEQUEATHED ALL PERTINENT WISDOM.
FROM THIS MOMENT ON, THIS MADNESS IS YOURS TO DO WITH AS YOU WILL...
NOVEMBER SWEEPS, HERE WE COME--
UMMM...DR. CLAIRE...?
SOMETHING... STRANGE UP ON THE CONTROL ROOM MONITORS.
YOU REALLY NEED TO SEE THIS...

TONIGHT--AN ENTERTAINMENT EXTRA EXCLUSIVE! WE'VE GOT CELEBRITY FOOTAGE YOU WON'T SEE ANYWHERE ELSE!
EXCLUSIVE VIRAL VIDEO COMING IN DIRECTLY FROM THE STILL-QUARANTINED MIDWAY CITY...
...A CELL PHONE CAMERA RECORDED THIS FOOTAGE FEATURING AN ELDERLY SUPERHERO CALLING HIMSELF "RISING SUN." THE IDENTITY OF THE VICTIM IS NOT YET KNOWN...
EXCLUSIVE FOOTAGE: MIDWAY CITY
PEOPLE OF THE WORLD--WHAT YOU ARE SEEING IS ONLY THE BEGINNING! AN APOCALYPSE OF YOUR OWN MAKING!
FIGHT FIRE WITH FIRE--!
...OUR APOLOGIES TO ANY VIEWERS WHO MIGHT BE...SENSITIVE TO THIS KIND OF VIOLENCE ON TELEVISION...
TO THOSE WHO AREN'T... L-LET'S SEE THAT ONE MORE TIME...
OFF AIR
FIGHT FIRE WITH FIRE--!
RISING SUN. HE BAITS US YET AGAIN.
THEN WHAT ARE WE WAITING FOR?
HOW THE HELL DID THIS GET ON TV?!

Y-YEAH...IT WAS *ME*...NO, I *SHOT* THE FOOTAGE ON MY VERY OWN PHONE...!
H-HEY... DON'T BLAME *ME*... BLAME MY *REP*. AT THIS POINT, THEY'LL RUN ANYTHING I *SEND* 'EM...
...YEAH, THERE'S MORE COMING. THIS GUY LIKES TO MAKE *SPEECHES*...!
I DUNNO...HE WANTS 'EM TO SEND IN THE *SUPERHERO MARINES* OR SOMETHING...!
THE AIR HERE STINKS OF OLD DEATH AND GODS WHO COULD NOT GET PROPER TRACTION.
LET THE WORLD WATCH AS WE EMBRACE *SPECTACLE* OVER...
...SUBSTANCE.
I *KNOW* THAT WONDER WAGON.

THAT'S...MIDWAY CITY...?!
IMAGINE IF THEY'RE HIDING JAPAN FROM US...
Then maybe we shouldn't even be here--
TOO EASY.
I WAS HOPING FOR MORE OF A CHALLENGE THE FIRST TIME OUT.
@MOSEXSBAT: FREEFALL AT 300 MPH. POWER DIVE. EXCELLENT.
about 6 seconds ago from Twitteratti

LISTEN, I KNOW IT SOUNDS CRAZY--! BUT I TOLD HIM ALL ABOUT HOW NEWS CYCLES WORK AND NOW--
BELIEVE ME, I'M KICKING MYSELF! I'M TOO GOOD AT THIS!
YOU'RE KIDDING! HE'S ALREADY GOT A Q-RATING?! HOW THE HELL--
I TRUST YOU'RE DOING YOUR JOB, HANOVER...
...BECAUSE THE WORLD NEEDS TO KNOW.
I'LL TAKE THEIR HYPOCRISY AND THROW IT RIGHT BACK IN THEIR FACES.
YOU'VE GOT THE WRONG ATTITUDE ON HYPOCRISY, OLD MAN--
--SOME OF US REVEL IN IT.
@MOSEXSBAT: THE GENERATION GAP HAS ITS BENEFITS.
about 2 seconds ago from Twitteratti

REVEL IN THIS.
YAH--!
NO WORRIES, TEAM--
--I'M OBSCENELY RICH AND I'M ALWAYS PREPARED.
@MOSEXSBAT: FIREPROOF CLOAK DISPENSER. STANDARD ISSUE.
about 2 seconds ago from Twitteratti
FINALLY! WE CAN BUST OUT ALL THE TRICKS!
A WALLY WEST SPECIAL. BACK WHEN HE WORE THE COOL KID FLASH COLORS.

INTOLERABLE DISRESPECT!
I'M NOT THE BROKEN MAN I ONCE WAS--I'VE FOUND MY PLACE IN THE NEW WORLD...!
THE LAST GASP OF A SENILE TROUBLE-MAKER--!
HA!

IT WASN'T LIKE THIS WITH THE DOLPHINS...
PSSST! HEY, AQUAZON...

...REMEMBER ME? YOUR FAVORITE PUBLICIST?
I KNOW I'VE LOOKED BETTER... BUT YOU WOULDN'T BELIEVE THE WEEK I'M HAVING...!

JUST WANTED TO LET YOU KNOW... THIS WHOLE RISING SUN P.R. PUSH... TOTALLY PRO BONO ON MY PART.
HE'S NOT A CLIENT OR ANYTHING.
HE JUST... Y'KNOW...SAID HE'D ROAST ME IF I DIDN'T HELP HIM SPREAD THE WORD...
IGNORANT WHELPS! I AM MORE THAN THE IZUMI YASUNARI YOU DISMISSED SO CASUALLY--
--SO MUCH MORE!
HE'S OBVIOUSLY NOT HIMSELF. RISING SUN WAS NEVER THIS CRAZED.
WE NEED A BETTER LOOK AT HIM. I NEED YOU TO ADJUST THE FREQUENCY OF YOUR CHEST BEAMER TO SOMETHING MORE INQUISITIVE RATHER THAN DESTRUCTIVE...
O-OKAY... YES...
LOLITA CANARY!
CAN YOU IMMOBILIZE HIM?
You only have to ask, Heino...
...I love yelling at old people.

SUMMMIIMASSENNN!!!
...NNNNNN...
GOT HIM. FULL BODY SCAN...
...YOU PICKING THIS UP?
INDEED. MY MOST EXCELLENT HANDHELD IS ATTUNED TO YOUR FREQUENCY.
Can you scan for insanity?
LIKE ALL CHILDREN...SO IGNORANT OF HISTORY. OF ALL THAT WHICH CAME BEFORE.
I HAVE FORGOTTEN MORE HEROIC SECRETS THAN YOU WILL EVER KNOW.
AND WHEN THE WORLD SEES THE FINAL SPIN ON THESE EVENTS... THE PEOPLE WILL LIONIZE ME--

--THEY WILL WORSHIP ME!
Yow--!
FIRE GOD COMPLEX. LET'S SEE IF HE'S GOT THE PHYSIOLOGY TO BACK IT UP--
--PERHAPS HE TRULY IS MORE THAN THE IZUMI YASUNARI WE DISMISSED SO CASUALLY.
@MOSEXSBAT: I'VE GOT MY META-WIKI ALL WARMED UP. READY TO POUNCE.
about 4 seconds ago from Twitteratti
AH, SO.
Wait.
What is that...?!
THERE IS A FOREIGN OBJECT LODGED WITHIN HIS CRANIUM.
@MOSEXSBAT: I KNEW RISING SUN WOULDN'T BE THIS MOTIVATED ON HIS OWN.
about 2 seconds ago from Twitteratti
So the old man's got help...

"...but what kind of help would put itself directly inside his brain?"

INSIDE RISING SUN'S BRAIN:

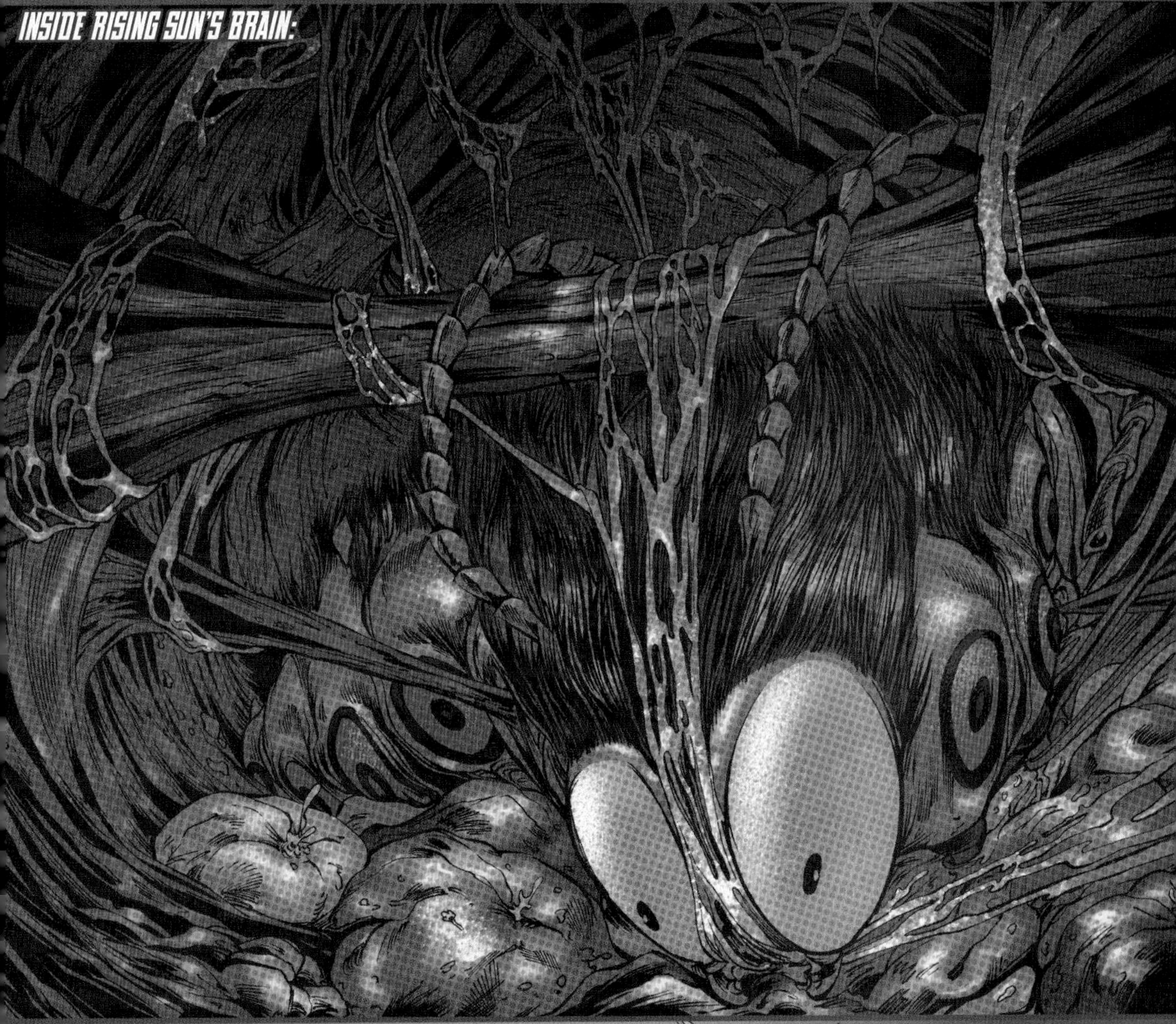

NEXT DANCE MOVE:

HEROES DIE.

LIVES FOREVER.

CHAPTER SIX

ChrisCross ▮ Penciller
Rob Stull with Marc Deering ▮ Inkers

PLASMAPHERESIS CONNECTION COMMUNITY SYSTEM ONLINE.
BETA-TESTING NEW TECHNOLOGY. NO NEED TO TYPE EVER AGAIN.
WELCOME TO THE NEW RAGE IN SOCIAL NETWORKING.
OUR MESSAGES CARRIED VIA PROTEIN MOLECULES DELIVERED DIRECTLY INTO A DIGITAL CENTRIFUGE. DISSEMINATED TO EVERYONE LOGGED INTO THE SYSTEM.
EVERYONE'S MINUTIAE ALL AT ONCE. MOMENT-TO-MOMENT NONSENSE. THE FOURTH STATE OF COMMUNICATION.
I INVENTED IT.
PREFERABLE TO CONSTANT, EXCLUSIVE TWEETS TO MYSELF.
I HAVE INSIGHT. I HAVE MONEY.
I AM MOST EXCELLENT SUPERBAT. WHAT ELSE NEEDS TO BE SAID?

SUPER MEGA FINALE:

MISTER MIND HAS FOUND A NEW HOME.

WELCOME TO *HAPPYLAND.*

NOT OF THIS EARTH, BUT SUBSUMED INTO WESTERN CULTURE. ONCE A PRISON OF AMUSEMENT-- NOW ALL OF *MIDWAY CITY* IS DARKSEID'S RUIN!

NOT THAT *YOU* WOULD KNOW! YOU HAVE *NO* SENSE OF *HISTORY!*

RISING SUN!
ONCE YOU WERE A RESPECTED HERO OF THE PEOPLE! YOU WERE A GLOBAL GUARDIAN! YOU WERE A MEMBER OF BIG SCIENCE ACTION! YOU HAD DIGNITY! YOU HAD FANS!
BLAME YOUR EXPANDING GUT ON WIDENING THE GENERATION GAP!
HE SPOKE IN RAMBLES. TWO VOICES OUT OF ONE MOUTH.
BUT OUR SCIENCE WAS FAR SUPERIOR TO HIS. WE WERE CLOSE TO UNCOVERING THE TRUTH.

YOU'VE GOT SOMETHING SPOOKY IN YOUR HEAD, OLD MAN!
SHINY HAPY AQUAZON: ON TAP.
BESIDES THE OBVIOUS BAD WIRING?
BIG ATOMIC LANTERN BOY: ON POINT.
He's got something to say--
SHY CRAZY LOLITA CANARY: ON GUARD.
WELL-SPOKEN SONIC LIGHTNING FLASH: ONLINE.
OUR HOMELAND IS A HOAX! SO MUCH EGO! SO MUCH PARANOIA!
THEY WANT A WESTERN ARMAGEDDON TO PULL FOCUS FROM THEIR EASTERN ONE!
YOU SHOULD'VE BROUGHT MORE CAMERAS!
THEY WANT THIS ON PRIME TIME!
MAKE IT QUICK, HEINO--
LANTERN BOY. I NEED TO GET INSIDE THAT MAN'S HEAD. I'VE GOT THE MAGIC JUICE...BUT YOU'VE GOT THE DELIVERY SYSTEM.
GET READY TO ADJUST YOUR CHEST BEAMER TO MY COMPUTATIONS...

I AM COMPELLED BEYOND REASON!
FIRE ONE--!
...DON'T KNOW HOW I'M GONNA SPIN THIS...HEROES VS. HEROES...
...I'VE GOT TWO BRANDS TEARING THEMSELVES APART--
--AND I'M GETTING IT ALL ON DIGITAL VIDEO--!?
REC
C'mon, Kim! Nap time's over!
This is where you show your father what for--!
WELL-SPOKEN SONIC LIGHTNING FLASH!
I NEED YOU TO PUT THE OLD MAN ON THE BULLET TRAIN!
ICAN DOTHAT BUTTHEN WHAT--?!
NO WORRIES. WE'VE GOT SOME OF OUR OWN TROPHIES NOW.
A WHITE DWARF SPECIAL. COURTESY OF THE BRAIN DRAIN...

...FOR THOSE HARD-TO-REACH PLACES.
UFFF--!
READY TO TAKE A LITTLE TRIP?
DEPENDS. WILL IT AFFECT MY SELF-ESTEEM?
ONLY IF SIZE MATTERS...
IT WAS POETRY IN MOTION. AND THEN HE TURNED HIS EYE TO ME.
I...AM... S-STILL...IN CONTROL--!
HAPPY TRAILS!
IN THAT MOMENT, WE FOUND A NEW MARKETING ANGLE--
--SUPER YOUNG TEAMWORK.

WE TARGETED ONE OF HIS TEAR DUCTS. THE QUICKEST WAY IN.
WE WERE THE STARS OF OUR OWN SUMMER BLOCKBUSTER.
I THOUGHT IT MIGHT BE MORE PROFOUND. LIKE STARING INTO THE ABYSS AND WONDERING WHAT MIGHT STARE BACK. BUT IT WASN'T LIKE THAT AT ALL...
...IT WAS A ROLLER COASTER RIDE FROM START TO FINISH.
PERFECT... IF YOU LIKE ROLLER COASTERS.
CAN'T HANG ON! HEINO--!
I... C-CAN'T HELP MYSELF--

--I STILL WANT YOU, KEIGO!

I HAVE ALWAYS WONDERED... IS MELODRAMA ITS OWN VIRTUE?
THE PIMPS AND THE POLITICIANS...THEIR IDEA OF CONTROL IS TO CONTROL THE LIES...!
TO CREATE THE LIES--!

WHATISHETALKINGABOUT...?
SOMETHING ABOUT PIMPING LIES, I THINK. NOT QUITE SURE.
MAYBE THE OLD DRUNK'S HAVING HIS MOMENT OF CLARITY...

THERE IS NO REAL THREAT... SAVE FOR THE THREAT WITHIN--!
THE FUTURE IS AT RISK--

--AND I CAN BURN IT ALL AWAY!

THAT'SOURCUE TOMOVE--
I HOPE THE OTHERS MADE IT... WHOOOAAAAA...
SOMEONE ONCE TOLD ME A FAMOUS QUOTE FROM GROUCHO MARX. SOMETHING ABOUT CLUBS AND THEIR MEMBERS. I HAD A CURIOUS REACTION...

...I SAID, "WHO'S GROUCHO MARX?"
NNNNN--
--NNNNOW WHAT...?
THIS... DOESN'T LOOK RIGHT...
WHERE'S SUPERBAT? THIS CAN'T BE--
FROM THE EDGES OF OUTER DARKNESS--

--LET THAT WHICH HAS BEEN LABELED MONSTER WAR II ERUPT INTO GLORY!
HERE, ON THIS BEACHHEAD, THE GHOULS AND THE GROTESQUES WILL BE FED THEIR OWN VIOLENT NIGHTMARES!
SO SPEAKS ULTIMON OF BIG SCIENCE ACTION!
KIM...IS THAT--
I...THINK IT IS. IT'S MY FATHER...
...BUT BACK WHEN HE WAS MY AGE! BACK WHEN HE WAS JUST JUNIOR WAVEMAN--!
TO ALL THE NEOPHYTES AND THE NAYSAYERS! THE AGE OF THE MEGA-HERO IS UPON US!
ALL PRETENDERS TO THE THRONE WILL BE INCINERATED WITHIN NUCLEAR FIRE! BURIED AT THE BASE OF MT. FUJI!
WE

NOT THIS ERA, DEAD ICON!
HE IS DEAD...ISN'T HE...?
FATHER--
--HOW ARE YOU PART OF THIS NIGHTMARE?!
THIS NIGHTMARE IS YOURS, CHILD.
FOR I HAVE NO DAUGHTER.
THESE YOUTH ARE A VIRUS! THEY INFECT THE FUTURE WITH TERMINAL IDEALS!
FOR THE PRESERVATION OF THE STATUS QUO--!
N-NO...I CANNOT...SUCCUMB TO THIS...INTRUSION...
...THIS INVASION OF SELF...!
LOOK...I THINK HE'S PULLING IT TOGETHER...

I AM... THE RISING SUN...!
I WAS A HERO... ONCE...
SHOULD WE BE WATCHING THIS? SEEMS LIKE A PRIVATE MOMENT...
ARE YOU SERIOUS--?!
YOU'RE RIGHT. HOPE SOMEONE'S FILMING IT...
I WILL ALWAYS BE THE YOUTH OF JAPAN! THE POSTER ON EVERY WALL--!
Y-YOU FORGOT YOUR BIKE, BOSS BOZO. LET ME SHOW YOU WHAT I CAN DO--
--*
GWHA--?!
C-CAN'T... SCREAM...?
LIFESTYLES COME AND GO, PHANTOM WAVEMAN--
THE TRUE PURPOSE OF WAR IS TO PRESERVE A WAY OF LIFE--
F-FATHER... DON'T--
SHOW BIZ IS IN MY BLOOD...

--BACK TO THE ABYSS WITH YOU!
...MY TALK SHOW APPEARANCES ARE SECOND TO NONE.

THINGS EMBEDDED WITHIN THE MIND. SUBCONSCIOUS PARTIES IN FULL SWING.
BUT WE HAD WORK TO DO. NO TIME FOR LOVE.
WE'RE NOT IN HARAJUKA ANYMORE.
BUT THERE'S NOTHING WORSE THAN BEING *OBVIOUS*.
PATENTED PERSONAL AIR SUPPLIES PROVIDED THE PERFECT MIXTURE. COMPRESSED OXYGEN WITH A HINT OF CINNAMON.

YOU GUYS CAN DEAL WITH YOUR INNER DEMONS SOME OTHER TIME.
THERE'S MORE FUN TO BE HAD IN *THIS* FUNHOUSE.
S-SO... WE *WEREN'T* FIGHTING THE OLD-TIMERS. WE'RE ACTUALLY *INSIDE*--
THIS IS OUR FINEST HOUR. WE'VE BECOME BACTERIA.
THIS IS WHAT SUPERHEROES DO...
...WE BREAK THROUGH BARRIERS. WE CONQUER PREJUDICE. WE RULE THE NIGHT.
AND NOTHING'S SHOCKING.
NOTHING AT ALL.
HEADS UP. I THINK I SEE...
...SOMETHING.
IT'S ALL CARBON DIOXIDE AND SULFURIC ACID! THAT'S MY NOSTALGIA!
THIS COCOON IS WET DEATH!

WH-WHAT... *IS* THAT--?!
COSMIC HYPERFLY.
WELL VERSED IN THE ART OF MIND CONTROL.
I ONCE TASTED EVERY UNIVERSE--
--AND I WILL AGAIN!
I'M JUST...A DRUNK FAILURE...
YOU'RE LETTING THAT SLUG GET TO YOU! IT SEES INSIDE YOUR **SOUL!**
YOU'RE *NOT* A DRUNK--
--YOU'RE CRAZY IN THE *BEST* WAY!

THESE SUPER-CONFRONTATIONS... THEY ALL END PRETTY MUCH THE SAME. THEY HAVE TO.
THEY'RE ALL THREE-CHORD POP SONGS.

THEY ALL REACH THE CRISIS POINT.

THEY'RE ALL DOUBLE-SIZED.
GAH--!
HNNGGGG--!

THEY'RE ALL PIN-UP OPPORTUNITIES.
ARE YOU READY TO RUMBLE?
TH-THIS IS ALL...TOO S-SOON...
I'M A... VENUSIAN SPACETIME CONQUEROR..
FAIR ENOUGH--

--BUT WE'RE NOT ON VENUS.

I'M TELLING YOU-- HE'S A HERO ON THE EDGE!
LOOK! LOOK--!
THERE IS...GREAT... NOBILITY...
SUPERHEROES ARE IDEAS LACED WITH IMMORTALITY.

WE CAN BE OUR OWN WORST ENEMY.
...B-BETTER... TO BURN OUT--
--THAN FADE AWAY!

WH-WHAT'S HAPPENING NOW?!
THE OLD MAN'S TAKING IT BACK! IT'S UP TO YOU, KIM--

BUT WHEN WE RISE FROM THE ASHES...

...EVERYONE BUYS A TICKET TO WATCH THE COMEBACK IN ACTION.

SHINY HAPPY AQUAZON HAD HER MOMENT.
PROTECTING US ALL FROM BEING DEEP FRIED AND PROVIDING THE KIND OF NARROW ESCAPE THAT TOTALLY GETS ME OFF.

BUT PERHAPS THE MOST PROFOUND THING I CAN SAY ABOUT SUPERHEROES IS SIMPLY THAT --
HOLD FEED.
SOMETIMES YOU FEEL LIKE A NUT...
ITAMI! I'M FEELING A LITTLE PARCHED...
YOUR MOST EXCELLENT MINERAL WATER, SIR.
LET'S TAKE A MOMENT TO SAVOR THE IRONY. WHO WOULD'VE THOUGHT IT WOULD END UP LIKE THIS...?
I KNOW YOU HAD PLANS. BUT IT WAS SO CLEAR WHERE YOUR LOYALTIES TRULY LAY...
INDEED, SIR.
NOW GO WASH THE WONDER WAGON FLEET.

WHO SAYS YOU CAN'T FIND GOOD HELP THESE DAYS...?
RESUME COMMUNITY ACCESS...
THEY FINALLY SENT IN THE JUSTICE LEAGUE TO CLEAN UP. AT LEAST, THEY SAID THEY WERE THE JUSTICE LEAGUE.
I DIDN'T RECOGNIZE ANY OF THEM.
THEY USED BIG WORDS LIKE "JURISDICTION" AND "RESPONSIBILITY" BEFORE THEY SCRAPED WHAT WAS LEFT OF RISING SUN OFF THE PAVEMENT.

I THINK THAT WAS THE MOMENT WHEN I REALIZED WHAT OUR TRUE PRIORITIES WERE. SUPER YOUNG TEAM WAS NOW A GLOBAL OPERATION, BUT THERE WAS STILL A HOME FIRE BURNING.
ALL THIS TIME THEY'D BEEN USING US TO DISTRACT THE WORLD FROM THE "CRISIS" IN JAPAN.

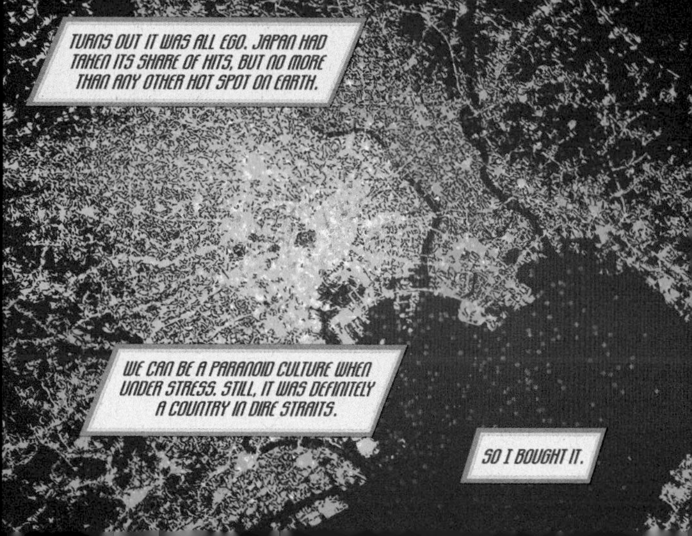
TURNS OUT IT WAS ALL EGO. JAPAN HAD TAKEN ITS SHARE OF HITS, BUT NO MORE THAN ANY OTHER HOT SPOT ON EARTH.
WE CAN BE A PARANOID CULTURE WHEN UNDER STRESS. STILL, IT WAS DEFINITELY A COUNTRY IN DIRE STRAITS.
SO I BOUGHT IT.

MADE THINGS MUCH EASIER. NOT TO MENTION... A LOT MORE FUN. JAPAN IN MY OWN IMAGE.
NO ONE HAS TO KNOW.
WITH THAT BIT OF NONSENSE OUT OF THE WAY, WE COULD ONCE AGAIN CONCENTRATE ON THE BUSINESS OF BEING FABULOUS.

OUR GLOBAL PRESS TOUR INCLUDED THE REQUISITE ENCOUNTERS WITH LOCAL SUPER-VILLAINS LOOKING TO CASH IN. WE KNOW HOW TO PLAY ALONG.
NOT SURE IF THE NEW MURDEROUS BEEFEATER IS READY FOR THE BIG LEAGUES YET. AT LEAST LANTERN BOY HAD FUN BLASTING HIM BACK TO A BYGONE TEA TIME.

KEIGO FOUND HIS CENTER BACK IN LAS VULGAR. HE POPS OVER EVERY CHANCE HE GETS TO LIVE IN THE MOMENT AND HIT THE TABLES WITH DOC DREAD AND OTHER LOCAL COLOR.
LIFE IS A GRAND GAMBLE.

CANARY FINALLY CASHED IN LIKE SHE ALWAYS WANTED TO.
YOU CAN VISIT A SHY CRAZY LOLITA CANARY SUPERSTORE IN ANY ONE OF SIX LOCATIONS GLOBALLY. THE TOKYO STORE IS HER HOME AWAY FROM HOME.
shy crazy lolita canary
superstore
SYT
SUPERSTORE
OPEN BAR EVERY NIGHT FROM SIX TO EIGHT.

KIM IS LIKE A WHOLE NEW AMPHIBIOUS FETISH FANTASY. STILL NOT MUCH OF A MULTI-TASKER, BUT SHE FINALLY KNOWS WHO SHE IS AND IT LOOKS GOOD ON HER.
SHE DOESN'T TALK TO HER FATHER ANYMORE.
WHEN OLD GHOSTS ARE FINALLY LAID TO REST--
PROXIMITY ALERT! LEVEL TWELVE TARGET ACQUIRED! UPLOADING COORDINATES!
AND, OCCASIONALLY, OUR FANS NEED TO SEE THEIR SUPERHEROES IN ACTION.
SO WE PLAY OUR PART...
ANOTHER MONSTER ATTACKING TOKYO, HEINO?
TOTALLY INCONVENIENT. I WAS ON MY WAY TO MEET WITH A NEW AGENT.
YOU KNOW THE DRILL, LANTERN BOY. ONE FOR THEM, ONE FOR US. AS OLD AS THE MYTHS WE NEVER BELIEVED IN...

SUPER YOUNG TEAM!
SUSPENSION OF DISBELIEF: OFF.
ONE DAY, MY BLESSED OFFSPRING WILL ASK ME WHO WON THE WAR.
I'LL TELL THEM WE OWN THE WAR.
WE CAN DO ANYTHING.
END